HINDSIGHT

A Story of Faith and Family

HINDSIGHT:
A STORY OF FAITH AND FAMILY

Katina Alami

To my seven children.

Table of Contents

Acknowledgements

I felt prompted to write this story in 2019 after our last adoption. There are many who were beneficial in getting this book to publishing; I desire to give credit where it is due.

First, my Heavenly Father who gave me this opportunity to grow and be refined. He inspired me to share this miraculous event with others. I am daily reminded of his mercy by my beautiful children.

Second, my husband Alan challenged me as I wrote. He guided my thinking and reminded me of details in several events. He helped make this story all that it is now.

Next, I want to thank my mother, Janie Spurlock, for her support and her faith that guided me and sustained me in this trial. Without her, I would have felt lost. She gave me roots to grow and nurtured my faith in the Savior.

I would also like to thank Sara, my children's caseworker, for her remarkable determination to help my children. She has been instrumental in their healing and overcoming obstacles in their lives. She put them first, when they were in foster care, and I'm grateful for her efforts.

Michelle and Octavio are beautiful people who were essential to this story. They played a part in helping my family come together. I am thankful for their mindfulness to hear and act upon the voice of the Lord. Their love towards my family will always be cherished.

Others, whose names I desire to mention, are Deanna Burns, Barbara Palmer, Amy Beaman, and Jessica Mortenson for taking the time to read, edit, photograph, or photoshop to make this book beautiful. These wonderful women stepped up to help when I asked. I am so grateful for their contributions.

I appreciate all those who took the time to read this book and give me their feedback, since October 2020, when <u>Hindsight: A Story of Faith and Family</u> was first published. I am grateful for each online review that has strengthened other's resolve to read my story. I appreciate those who have shared this book with friends, family, or co-workers. This book has touched so many lives. I pray that it continues to be an example of how to hear the voice of the Lord.

Katina Alami

CHAPTER 1

No Other Way

Most people told me to relax, it would happen. Pregnancy took time and we had only been trying for a year. They didn't understand though. Something was wrong.

When I was fourteen, my mother, Janie, had taken me to a specialist who was set up at the health department in my rural town of Prestonsburg, Kentucky. I had started my period, but was irregular. My mother, fearing for my health, sought out a medical answer for that irregularity. I was questioned—both in front of my mother and privately. I was fourteen. It felt more like an interrogation than asking for my medical history. Their biggest accusation was, "You're a teenager. You must be sexually active." Um. No. I was a *good* Christian girl. I couldn't look a boy straight in the eyes let alone have sex with him at that age! I was met with skepticism and

unbelief from everyone in the room, except my mother.
She knew I was telling the truth. I felt so peculiar up
against these medical professionals. I wasn't normal for
waiting for marriage to have sex. The doctor did not
seem to hear my mother's correction: I needed treatment
for my menstrual irregularity. I wasn't pregnant and
didn't need a prescription for sex protection! Regardless,
he recommended that I take birth control and handed
me a paper bag containing a twelve month's supply of
pills. I threw them in the trash outside the health
department. I was convinced they were of the devil and I
would never *need* to take them.

　　Fast forward ten years; my husband, Alan, and I
tried for six months to become pregnant without success.
Alan and I agreed we had made an appropriate effort; it
was probably time for me to see a doctor. I did research
online and sought out an appointment with a nearby
gynecologist in Lexington, Kentucky. The visit was
anything but comfortable.

　　I sat in the waiting area surrounded by many
pregnant women. I was filled with jealous anger
imagining that those women didn't realize what they
had. Pregnancy had come naturally and easily for them—
I assumed. Feeling like I was the anomaly in the room,
my fears and frustrations took hold. I sat in silence,
envying those expectant mothers.

　　My name was called. My turn. An ultrasound was
done by Dr. Day, which took less than a minute. She had

scarcely moved the device long enough to see anything when she looked at me with wide eyes and said, "I think you need to see a specialist; I suspect you have Premature Ovarian Failure." She handed me a list of fertility doctors and suggested that I call one of them for an appointment. I asked her to explain, but she denied my request. Indicating that she didn't have the professional expertise to diagnose me, she worried that she could be wrong. I needed a specialist.

I cried in my car as I tried to make sense of our conversation. What did that mean for me going forward? I had dreamed of becoming a mother since childhood. I loved taking care of children, cuddling on them, and teaching them. I loved being domestic—sewing, crafting, and cooking. Most of all, I loved the idea of being able to be like my Heavenly Father—a co-creator with Him and the understanding of how to purely love another. I needed to overcome this; I needed the Lord to show me how. I feared my dream was slipping away from me. I felt entitled to be a mother. It was my right as a woman. Dr. Day had not provided an explanation, diagnosis, or treatment plan—just a suspicion. I was left with more questions than answers.

One thing I knew. I had to trust in God. I had felt His Spirit prompt me many times before to do certain things—like when my parents had bought me an old 1998 Ford Escort for my sixteenth birthday. It was a nice car and not too expensive for a new driver who ran the risk of totaling it every time I drove. I had come home from school one afternoon and parked my pride and joy in our four-car-wide driveway. I ran inside and dropped off my school books in my upstairs bedroom. I had the thought come to me, "Move your car." I felt the Spirit warm my heart and wondered if this was what the Holy Ghost felt like. Regardless of how silly it is to listen to a voice in your head, I immediately ran outside to move it to the other side of the driveway that partially wrapped around the house. No sooner had I done this and dropped my keys back on the hook by the door, my Uncle John pulled up in his pickup truck right in front of where I had first parked my car minutes before. I yelled for my dad and decided to join him outside. Before my uncle could walk around his car, it started rolling—backwards! Gasping, my dad and uncle ran after it. Crash! The hill behind my house had stopped the car from rolling any further. In hindsight, had I not listened to the voice of the Spirit and moved my vehicle, it would have been collateral damage along the pickup's path. I immediately said a prayer of gratitude. I knew God had warned me to move my car.

This experience was one instance of how I learned to listen to the promptings of the Holy Ghost. Now, sitting in the parking garage of a gynecologist's office, I wanted His voice again to tell me what to do. I recalled the words of a favorite primary song: "Pray, He is there. Speak, He is listening. You are His child. His love now surrounds you."[1] I sang this song as I drove home. It had

---

1 From A Child's Prayer © 1984 Janice Kapp Perry. Used by permission.

always brought me relief during times of adversity. I had faith that the Lord would fix this heartache somehow. Yet, I felt like I had entered a dark room and was stumbling around unable to find the light. I prayed for comfort.

As I prayed, I made a commitment to God to live more righteously. I was going to do anything and everything so the Lord could not withhold his blessings from me. I immersed myself more frequently in scripture study—exercising my faith in God that He would help me see what to do through His words.

I didn't call anyone on the list of specialists Dr. Day had given me right away. Alan was seeking a management position at his company and that position came with a risk of moving, even out of state. Alan and I both agreed before we were married that I would stay home with the children and he would be the breadwinner for our family. Remembering that agreement, and knowing we would need this promotion in order to feed little ones, I put off seeing a specialist so I could find one near our new residence—wherever that would be.

Within a few months, Alan was successful in his promotion. Having faith that this move would help us, and praying to confirm this move was directed by the Lord, we packed our apartment and moved to Louisville, Kentucky. It was exciting for us because we didn't have to move far. It was only an hour away from both of our families. Later in my life, I would recognize how this move was a tender mercy from the Lord—truly an answered prayer. I did not foresee at the present time how this move would fortify my marriage and was the key to growing my family.

A few months later, in September 2012, we were settled in a new apartment and new job offices. Alan managed a rental-car location and I worked next door as an optician, which happened to be in the same shopping plaza—a coincidence that we counted as a miracle itself. Becoming comfortable in our new locations, Alan and I agreed it was time to get a second opinion from a fertility specialist. We longed for a child and the months after our move still hadn't resulted in pregnancy. Although, I had hoped they would have.

We sought the help from the best fertility specialist an hour north of Louisville in Cincinnati, Ohio. I nervously sat with my feet in stirrups in preparation for another ultrasound. I was hopeful that we would finally receive some answers. I was sure that the Lord would inspire this doctor to tell me some good news. I had prayed and read my scriptures daily. I was being faithful and righteous. Surely the Lord would deliver us out of this trial.

Dr. Smith quickly administered the ultrasound, but became silent as he looked at Alan and I. Stillness. No words. It seemed like hours had passed in a matter of minutes. We knew his thoughts before he had even spoken them aloud. My diagnosis was as the previous doctor had suspected—Premature Ovarian Failure.

Grief swept over my husband and I. We were told that I had no eggs; my body had emptied all that I had years earlier. I was going through menopause at age twenty-six. I was also diagnosed with osteopenia, the onset of osteoporosis. To keep my body functioning at my actual age and to not deteriorate further, the doctor placed me on birth control.

My mind raced back to that day at the health department. I remembered stuffing those pills with such emotion into the trash. Ten years later, I *needed* them. It seemed strange to be in a different position now. I would need estrogen to keep myself healthy until I was 40, with bone density scans every few years. It was essential to my wellbeing. I fell into shock. My ears, heart, and mind went numb and I stopped listening to the doctor as he tried to explain. He confirmed: I had a chronic illness that would hinder my dream of motherhood.

I thought, "This could not be. This is not happening to me! I have done everything the Lord has ever asked me to do. I went to seminary, served a full-time mission, graduated from college, got married in the temple, and am trying to be a mother. I have done everything right. I have followed all the steps! Surely, I am entitled to the blessing of motherhood because I have done all these things. Why is this happening? This isn't right." These thoughts buzzed in my mind like a radio that just wouldn't turn off. I couldn't get past it. I felt lost, betrayed by the Lord, and useless. I was taught that motherhood was the ultimate crowning glory of womanhood and I felt like I was losing my purpose.

At twelve years old I had received my Patriarchal Blessing, a special prayer-like blessing that is given to reveal inspired direction for a person's life from the Lord.[2] In this blessing I was promised that I would be a mother to *many* children. I questioned the Lord and his promises because, in my eyes, my plan had become "frustrated."[3]

Over time the feelings of grief turned into hopelessness and desperation. Genetic testing had proved I was normal and there was no discoverable cause for my early menopausal state. Remembering what I had been taught about faith, I had to humble myself before the Lord[4] and rely on Him for the promised blessing I wanted. However, I knew that *faith* was a proactive word, not a passive one. I knew I would have to work for what I desired, so I began researching adoption agencies and costs.

It was difficult to be proactive in this research. I still felt the Lord's betrayal. It was a wound on my heart that was digging away at my faith. Every doubt that had

---

[2]'Gospel Topics, 'Patriarchal Blessings, https://www.churchofjesuschrist.org/study/manual/gospel-topics/patriarchal-blessings?lang=eng, (25 January 2020).

[3] Doctrine & Covenants 3:1

[4] James 4:10

brought me to my knees pleading for understanding was left unassured. Those doubts pulled at my soul. I felt as though pieces of me were being erased every time my prayers seemed to be ignored—like I was unworthy of the Lord's time. Yet, I had felt the Lord's power in my life. I knew he was real and would answer my prayers on His timetable. So, as I lingered in my darkness, I pressed forward with an adoption application. It was my way of being proactive, exercising faith, and pushing through my grief. Faithful proactiveness meant using all of my earthly knowledge to find a way to become a mother. When the time was right, the Lord would reveal the heavenly knowledge I needed to fulfill His promises.

Alan grieved our loss in a different way. He fought me with stubbornness. He had quickly come to terms with our reality. He had the idea that, if we couldn't have children naturally, then children weren't for us. He confessed that underneath his outward facade was fear. Not being able to have a biological child brought a risk for him. He feared not being able to love a child that was not biologically his, a notion that I had never considered.

His other fear was cost. We knew it was going to be expensive, and we felt discouraged learning how much of our savings we would have to deplete. One agency promised us a child for $25,000 if we adopted domestically, and $65,000 for international children. Even with adoption as our only choice, there was no way Alan and I could afford more than one child. Even a single domestic adoption would require us to sacrifice and live meagerly. I understood; his fears were valid. We weren't financially able to do this.

I had imagined motherhood my entire life. I hungered for it. He dismissed my pleas for adoption multiple times due to these fears. I couldn't blame him. Yet, I couldn't give up either. How was I going to convince my husband this was the only option for us? Would we ever be able to afford one child without it feeling like a financial burden? In my young mind, there was no other way that I could feel satisfied. I needed to be a mother.

Through all this doubt and fear I kept trying to act. I was desperately searching for a way out of my misfortune. I filled out the paperwork and forced Alan to sign it with the idea that we could simply learn about the process, so when the time came to do it, we would be ready.

CHAPTER 2

Stereotypes

A few months earlier, due to Alan's promotion, we had been stressfully hunting for an apartment in Louisville. Popular complexes either had waitlists a mile long or were immensely overpriced. Alan and I spent hours on a Saturday a few weeks before our move touring various apartment communities near our new work offices.

After viewing options in our price range, we took a minute to pray about each unit. The Lord had made it clear to us that He wanted us to live in Louisville, but we wondered if He had a specific complex in mind for us. He did. We felt the Spirit warm our hearts and guide us to choose one of the communities at the top of our price range. Uneasy of how tight our money would be if we chose that specific apartment, we prayed again.

Immediately we felt the confirmation to go put our name on a lease. We faithfully did.

Our first apartment was in the Hillview suburb of Louisville. The Church of Jesus Christ of Latter-day Saints is a worldwide church, so it is necessary for members to be divided into smaller congregations according to their place of residence. Hillview was mostly assigned to the Louisville Sixth Ward congregation; however, our apartment complex was cut out like a square convex in the boundary and assigned to the Louisville Fourth Ward building. Our suburb, where we had spent hours looking for a place to live, was attending an entirely different ward except for the complex Alan and I chose to move into. We often wondered about this unique boundary line.

Going to church the first Sunday after our move, I was caught off guard. I had imagined a modern building with red brick, a white steeple, and white metal doors with frosted glass inserts—much like the ward building we had moved away from. We pulled up off Dixie Highway and the entire building was brown. It was an older building that had been built in the late seventies, early eighties. It had brown bricks, gutters, and trim, with a brown steel steeple. On either side of the brown metal entrance doors were two large cream-colored globe lights.

Memories of my pre-teen and teenage years came flooding to my mind. I spent those years living in the hills of eastern Kentucky. The building I attended in my youth, the Martin Ward, was set up on a hill. Similar to the Louisville Fourth Ward building, it too was built in the early eighties and had the same brown theme.

I was the only active young woman my age at church during those years. I really didn't have many friends because the girls were older or younger than me; mostly, my cousins or sister's friends. The boys close to my age, I couldn't talk to. They were boys after all. I was extremely awkward, yet eager to fit in with the other girls. Sometimes I made immature or inappropriate choices, simply to be like them. It didn't matter; at home, school, or church, I was tasteless and unrefined. It wasn't a very happy time in my life. A reminder of that bleakness as we attended church that first Sunday was not very comforting to me.

I had felt the Spirit confirm in my heart that we were supposed to be in Louisville, but moving to this ward was frustrating. I often wondered how I was to move forward when I was dealing with grief from infertility, away from family, and didn't have any friends in Louisville to help me cope. Then I met Rebecka.

Rebecka was a mom of four foster children who attended the Louisville Fourth Ward. She and her husband were in the same position as we were. They desired to have children, but were unable to have them naturally. They had decided to foster children and ended up with some really great kids. One Sunday she lingered to talk to me after church. Having listened to my complaints and desires concerning motherhood, she felt prompted to tell me to look into foster care. She asked Alan and I to pray about it. This was how the Lord was blessing her to become a mother. Perhaps the Lord wanted us to foster too. Rebecka had empathy for me.

Foster care was out of the question for us. We didn't want to end up with kids that had *something wrong with them*. We heard many stereotypes about foster kids. It just didn't feel right. I didn't want to end up with a problem child. While some people could handle special needs children, we couldn't. I knew our weaknesses—Alan's and mine. We felt like we would be very unhappy if we chose to adopt kids with medical or emotional problems that would require more of our time and attention. We wanted *normal* children.

I dismissed her ideas and continued to pursue my adoption route through an agency. In retrospect, I am thankful to the Lord for the tender mercy of placing us in the Fourth Ward. Rebecka—dear, sweet Rebecka— was softening my heart without my knowledge. She was breaking down those stereotypes to which Alan and I clung. But meeting Rebecka wasn't the only blessing we found in Fourth Ward.

Through a beautiful family whom we had met at church, Alan was given a chance to change careers selling health and life insurance benefits. We prayed and received that familiar stir from the Holy Ghost in our hearts which confirmed this job change was what God wanted us to do. It was a test of faith. At the rental car company, Alan had potential for continued advancement. He could become a general or regional manager, and pursue the hierarchy within the business. If Alan decided to take this new job, there wasn't going to be many openings for advancement. He knew he was going to be stuck at a desk for several years.

Alan is not the type of person that likes to sit still. His mind is always moving. He likes to dabble in a lot of different things, and when he gets bored or learns as much as he can about one topic, he moves on to the next. To take a job, where he would certainly become stuck for a time, didn't sit well with him. But he also knew the promptings of the Spirit. We both knew that when God commands, one must "go and do."[5] He began studying to take insurance licensing tests.

My parents communicated to me their concerns during this time. They were skeptical of all the big decisions we were making. We had moved away from them to Louisville, switched careers a few months after we got there, and were pursuing an adoption that we could barely afford. These choices appeared foolish to them. They worried we were trapping ourselves; for they also knew Alan could never be happy in a job like this one. My dad had firsthand experience.

After getting a college major in Communications, my dad sought to find a job in radio, television, or advertisement. He was disappointed to find that getting

---

[5] 1 Nephi 3:7

work in any of those fields was difficult. He didn't feel like he could support our family as he tried to find work; therefore, he took what came to him. He eventually got into the life insurance business. He worked for many years with various companies, and he became proficient in the ways of selling insurance policies. However, my dad felt trapped. He didn't wish those same feelings or circumstances on any of his children. Yet, the Lord was calling us into the very career that my father had warned us about many times over.

Despite my father's counsel, we relied on our faith in the Savior and the feelings from the Spirit to guide us. Alan and I prayed he would pass the insurance tests, which he did, and he started a new position as a benefits specialist. I also had a career change during this time. I was able to put my teaching certificate to good use and taught intervention classes in the public-school system. During the summer, I worked at the same optometry office that I had transferred to when coming to Louisville. It was a season of changing for the better, and each of these changes was a stepping stone needed to obtain the blessings we desired.

In only five months, we were able to add enough to our savings for a down payment on a house. Our money would now work to build equity instead of dissipating into apartment rent. The Lord was guiding us as we accomplished this personal goal. We needed the space to grow our family. We had faith that when the moment was right, He would provide the children we sought.

CHAPTER 3

Effort

In the course of our efforts to bring children into our home, it was hard to see how any of the decisions we made would help meet this goal. Yet, every decision Alan and I made were stepping stones to something greater. Faith is something that I had with *every* choice. I chose to do whatever my Heavenly Father commanded. I trusted Him. Although sometimes what He wanted seemed pointless and counterproductive to my desires, I let Him take the lead in my life. We had focused on our careers, obtaining more money, and spending money on a house, which was strange to me. I felt like I was trading my future children for "treasures [on] earth,"[6] and it seemed out of sync with what the Savior taught about

---

[6] Matthew 6:19-20

the worth of children.[7] However, certain things were needed in order to bring Alan and I closer to building our family.

Someone wise once said, "If at first you don't succeed try, try again."[8] Thus, I began creating an online adoption profile. We decided to adopt through Latter-Day Saint Family Services as a way to cut down on some of the costs. Because of our membership in The Church of Jesus Christ of Latter-Day Saints, we would only be required to pay ten percent of the total cost of the adoption. Birth mothers used the LDS Family Services website to access pictures and biographies of adoptive couples in order to choose parents for their child. I worked tirelessly on our profile. I created social media groups that linked to it and designed business cards. I was determined to have the most colorful and attractive profile; birth mothers would not be able to pass us up when scrolling through numerous couples! It was hard work, yet my dedication eased my grief. I was being proactive, exercising my faith, and found purpose in this project.

Before our profile could be published, we had to take some online parenting classes, undergo a home study, and meet with adoption caseworkers. I became discouraged when I learned there were two parenting

---

[7] Matthew 19:14

[8] 'Well-Known Expressions', *Book Browse*, https://www.bookbrowse.com/expressions/detail/index.cfm/expression_number/586/if-at-first-you-dont-succeed-try-try-again, (7 October 2019).

classes Alan and I would need to purchase and take. It would cost us $250 total.

Alan is a skilled money manager; he has always handled the finances in our marriage. He knows the value of a dollar, and always has lived as frugal as he can to accomplish his financial goals. He tucks money into various savings accounts and invests in stock. He enjoys giving advice to his friends, family, and coworkers as they plan for retirement. It's quite amazing to me how well he plans for our financial future. However, being money-wise means carefully calculating what expenses are of *value.* Since Alan wasn't fully on-board with pursuing adoption, I was hesitant to ask him to spend $250 on classes. On the other hand, I couldn't progress further in the adoption process without discussing this financial decision with him. I felt stuck.

He had watched me patiently as I struggled with my grief. Passively, Alan had let me pursue this adoption without comment. He dealt with his grief by having a positive attitude and faith. He felt the Lord had allowed this to happen, so being childless at that time was what the Lord wanted for us. However, I felt like I couldn't stop. I was like an archer with my eye fixated on the target. I could not be distracted. This was our family— our future children! I had to keep going. I recognized our infertility was more than a proclaimed fate from the Lord, it was an obstacle that the Lord had power to help us overcome. I wanted Alan to understand—he just had to!

I wondered how this conversation would go. Would Alan see this needed to be done? Would he support me? What would I do if he didn't? I prayed the Lord would help me as I debated my desire with my husband.

I approached him after work one evening. Our dialog went something like this:

"I worked on our adoption profile today," I began casually.

"Cool," he replied.

"The next step is to publish it."

"Awesome."

I carefully continued, "Before we can do that, we have to commit to do a few things. We have to take some classes, do a home study, and meet with a case worker. The classes cost $125 for each of us." I paused to let him consider what I was asking of him.

To my astonishment, Alan replied, "Honey, if it makes you happy, do it."

I hadn't known what to expect going into that conversation. I was positive it was going to end in a fight. It was the first actual moment I had heard any verbal support for the efforts I was making. It made my heart leap that I might in fact succeed. I might actually be a mom through adoption. Alan's heart was softening. He still acted as a spectator in the process, but I couldn't help but thank the Lord for this mutual agreement.

I paid for the online classes and logged into his account and took his for him. Alan did not have a sense of urgency in this matter and I doubted he would complete these classes on his own, so I broke the rules. I was glad I did. This enabled us to meet with a caseworker sooner.

A month later we drove to Lexington, Kentucky where the closest LDS Family Adoption Services representative was located. He told us the next steps to become eligible adoptive parents, and gave us some pointers on how to advertise ourselves to birth mothers. Yes, we had to advertise ourselves to those who were giving us their child. I found it difficult to comprehend. It seemed wrong almost, like I was begging them for their baby. I pushed away these feelings. Everyone who had been in my position had to do this, and now I had to figure out how we would do it.

***

A month later I paused in my profile-creating efforts. Since we had saved enough money for a down-payment on a house, it became necessary to make house hunting our priority. I was eager to switch my vision, because we would need a bigger home to expand our family. From the Louisville suburb of Hillview to the suburb of Buechel (twenty minutes east and closer to Alan's new work office), we moved from our one-bedroom apartment into a three-bedroom, one-bath house—the perfect size for a family just starting out.

Unpacking took time as Alan and I juggled our new jobs and organizing the new house. Yet before I could get back to creating our adoption profile, Alan and

I received some discouraging news. After many years of operation, LDS Family Services had decided to discontinue adoptions.

I became discouraged, angry, and frustrated. I sobbed that night as I knelt by my bedside to pray. I slammed my fists onto the bed, furious at heaven. I wanted to know one thing: *Why?* I pleaded with God to give me a window because He had closed my door. But He hadn't simply closed it; He had slammed it in my face! Again, my faith was being tested.

I felt out of options. We had depleted our savings for the down payment on our house. There was no money to go elsewhere. I would have to wait at least a year before the money was saved up again to go through a different agency. Even then, there would be a long period of waiting until we were chosen by birth parents. I couldn't wait. I felt an unexplainable compulsion to be a mother now.

I paused in my prayer to listen for the Spirit. What did God have to say for Himself? As I waited for an answer, He brought peace to my heart. He assured me to have faith in His promises, be patient, and "all things shall work together for [my] good."[9] He would help me to see what to do next. I had to trust the peaceful whispering of the Spirit. He would show me the way even when I was disheartened, depressed, and

---

[9] Doctrine and Covenants 90:24

disappointed. I decided to "try, try again."[10]

[10] 'Well-Known Expressions', *Book Browse,*
https://www.bookbrowse.com/expressions/detail/index.cfm/expression_number/
586/if-at-first-you-dont-succeed-try-try-again, (7 October 2019).

CHAPTER 4

Aubrey

It was difficult to process the closing of our agency. I wondered if this was a sign from God, or if adoption was not what the Lord wanted us to do. I questioned the existence of God at one point, because I believed a loving God wouldn't put his children through such heartache. During those moments of doubt, I remembered my personal experiences. I had felt the Spirit, or so I thought. Motherhood was a righteous desire, and I had served my Heavenly Father to the best of my ability. I wondered: Was He listening to me? Where was His hand pouring out his blessings? I had been acting on what I thought he wanted me to do; so, where was my reward?

I had the misconception that God would simply give me the blessings I asked for, if I was righteous enough. I pondered on these things while I tried to determine how to move forward. Desperate to have answers, I clung to the faith that I had in Jesus Christ. I had felt His comforting power. Deep in my soul I knew it. When all my plans had failed, I was ready to devise another. I was willing to sacrifice all of our material possessions to gain the children that we had been promised. Somehow, we would overcome this.

When we bought our first house, our church building assignment changed. We left the Fourth Ward and entered the Louisville Sixth Ward. It was a larger ward with lots of young families.

My bitterness due to LDS Family Services closing their adoption doors was hard to mask as I became acquainted with those in my new ward. I was testier than I should have been with people at church—jealous of their budding parentage. Each complaint I heard from new or experienced mothers made me want to scream. I impatiently would say, "I don't know about that because I can't have children." My response made me feel vindicated, but made it harder for me to form friendships. Yet through it all, they warmly opened their hearts to us and seemed glad to have us in their company.

During this transition between wards, I couldn't shake the conversation that I had with Rebecka. I still visited her often and babysat her children. I saw firsthand how wonderful and *normal* her foster kids were! They were kind, loving, and playful.

Months after our move I kept revisiting my thoughts on foster care. I researched how to become a foster parent and how many children in our state needed adoptive families. Doing this research and interacting with Rebecka's children brought a change in my heart; my thoughts about foster care were changing. Maybe this was the window the Lord was opening.

I was ready. I laid down my fears and picked up my faith. My new plan was to take foster parent training classes and see what it was all about. I needed to know more. How were we to make a decision about something if we didn't have all the information? Alan consented. He indicated he had felt a prompting from the Spirit. We both felt this could be beneficial for us.

We attended an informational meeting the following week. I was nervous. The social workers that spoke wanted everyone who attended to become foster parents; for they were, and still are, sorely needed. Most in the room, like us, wanted a baby; however, the workers were upfront with us: The odds of getting a baby from the foster system aren't good. Typically, a baby comes with a set of older siblings, or you have to know someone within the system. Babies are in high demand for fostering to adopt parents.

I felt discouraged. There were many older children in the foster system and these speakers were asking us to consider them. I was skeptical that I could help an older child. Alan and I were a young couple. I didn't want our child to be older than the four years we had been married! I felt weird about that—like people would judge us for the sin of having a child out of wedlock, although that wasn't the case. I also knew that the older the child, the harder it would be to help the child overcome any misguided behaviors from birth parents.

There were plenty of other worries too: How would we deal with birth parent visitation? Court orders? I thought it would be hard to be a parent when the Division of Child and Behavioral Health Services (DCBHS or the State) would have ultimate authority over each child. Above all, we were seeking to adopt, but the primary goal for foster children is reunification with birth family, not adoption. I couldn't fathom the idea of sending a child back to birth parents who had abused them.

We left the meeting feeling overwhelmed and wondering if we could meet the challenges of these kids. Would becoming foster parents even help us achieve our goal of adoption? We discussed all these things on the car ride home. Could this really be what the Lord was calling us to do?

***

Monday nights are designated in our home as Family Home Evening. Alan and I would take that time together and usually read scriptures. We discussed what we thought about what we read and how we could apply those teachings into our lives. We carved out that time during the week to "check-in" with one another and align our schedules. It was a time both of us looked forward to. It strengthened our marriage and kept us focused on our financial, emotional, and spiritual goals in life.

At the informational foster care meeting, we had noticed that the State taught training classes every Monday night. We both thought it was a perfect opportunity since we were already setting aside that time for the two of us each week. Like so many times before, we recognized the Lord's hand and stirrings of the Holy Spirit in our chests. If He didn't want us to do it, we had faith that He would help us feel that we should stop. Despite our worries, we put our trust in Heavenly Father.

Over the next few months, July and August, Monday nights were spent in downtown Louisville at the Cabinet for Health and Family Services getting certified as foster parents. Since adoption was our goal, rather than traditional foster parenting, we chose to be designated as a concurrent planning home—a fancy name for the foster to adopt program.

Each class inched us closer to certification. Although this was exciting for both Alan and I, week after week we were met with a new, hard-hitting topic of discussion. We conversed about how children normally develop, and how those with trauma develop differently. We learned about the types of trauma that cause children to end up in foster care. We were asked to role play situations children face daily, so we could try to understand the various sufferings that foster children encounter and how to parent a child who has endured them. I had been sheltered as a child, and I felt exposed and uncomfortable at these sessions. I got a taste of how evil the world could be. It was heartbreaking to imagine a young child being exposed to the things we spoke of each week; things like sex, violent crimes, physical and emotional neglect, various forms of abuse, or the horrors of drug addiction. It was hard to listen to stories about the boy who hoarded food under his bed, the toddler who slept in a dog cage littered with feces, or the girl who was forced, by her parents, to eat her own vomit. I sometimes would cry; I wanted to be a mother, but the thought of a child being put in such horrific circumstances before they could come to me was deeply saddening.

By the end of August, we were certified foster parents. I trusted in the Lord that He would instruct us what to do next. It became a period of waiting on Him.

We had a home study done and met with our caseworker, Holly. She was a nice woman but seemed very skeptical of us. Holly wasn't sure we could handle the demands of foster children. When she asked us why we wanted to become foster parents, her skepticism seemed to deepen. We were still experiencing some serious grief over infertility, and we didn't try to hide it. She asked us questions about our marriage relationship, extended family relationships, and devoutness to our religion. We watched nervously at her flickering pen as she made notes about the comments we made, the opinions we had, and our mannerisms as we talked. When our background check and home study came back with no issues, we were thankful. Our names were placed on the list of open homes and then we waited, waited, and waited.

Our first call came in October 2014. I can't describe how hard it is to make a decision that could affect your family for eternity in a matter of a few minutes. Placement caseworkers start calling foster parents on a list of open homes. They keep calling potential homes until someone picks up and accepts the child for placement. Each time a description and some information about the child is given. Every phone call was a test of faith. I prayed to the Lord each time, "Is this *my* child? Am I supposed to help this one?"

We were offered a two-year-old little boy with some behavioral issues. He had been known to be defiant and was diagnosed with RAD (Reactive Detachment Disorder). He had been passed around so frequently in his two years of life that he had not developed healthy attachments to his caregivers.

At that time, Alan and I both felt like it wasn't something we could do. This child had unresolved problems and I felt my human weakness like a weight. I knew I couldn't handle him, so out of love, we reluctantly declined. The Lord had brought us to this point: to be foster parents. Regardless of the training I had, I still felt ill equipped to care for these kids the way they needed to be cared for. I knew the Lord would only ask me to do things that I was capable of accomplishing. So, with faith, I stuck to my decision and pushed away the guilty feelings I had from rejecting this little boy. He wasn't meant to be mine.

Another phone call didn't come until December for another two-year-old boy. He was exactly the type of child we had been waiting for. He didn't have any behavior problems, no mental health concerns, or medical conditions. His need for placement stemmed from neglect by his birth parents.

I asked if I could call the placement worker back. I called Alan at work and we prayed together over the phone. Again, we didn't feel good about this placement. We couldn't feel the familiar warmth of the Holy Spirit telling us to proceed. Holly called me after I had refused this child also. She frustratingly asked, "Will you ever take children?" It was a hurtful remark and I couldn't tell her why we had refused. It was something that I didn't think she would understand. I wearily took her words to heart: Was she right; would we ever take children? If we didn't, what was the purpose of all this?

Over the next month Alan and I struggled with this idea. We had been approved since the end of summer and had not accepted a single placement. I wondered: What was wrong with us? Why did we not feel inclined to take any children? Why was the State not calling us more frequently? Did we offend them from our last phone call? Alan and I talked about these thoughts regularly.

The holidays came and went as we pondered. It had been four months since we were officially a foster home. We wondered why the State claimed to have all these children in need of homes, yet we kept thinking our home was being overlooked.

January 14, 2015 was a day that I will never forget. I had just gotten home from teaching at school. I was preparing dinner when I received a placement call. Our paperwork we signed with the State granted them permission to call us with children ages zero through two. I was surprised to discover we were being asked to take a five-year-old girl. The worker stated her name was Aubrey and she had been looking for a placement home for a few hours. I felt in that moment what I had been waiting for—a feeling I was unsure would ever come. The Spirit burned within my heart. I was stunned. I quickly speculated how I could take a five-year-old? She had already been taught poor behaviors and I could foresee a struggle in order to change them. I questioned why the Lord was asking this of me. Again, I hadn't let go of those stereotypes.

I immediately told the woman on the other end of the phone that I needed to call my husband. I asked her, "Please wait a few minutes before you call anyone else." She agreed. Alan quickly answered his phone at work. I told him about Aubrey and how God was touching my heart.

He answered, "I think you may be right." We prayed together over the phone. The feelings we both experienced in that prayer were so powerful we could not doubt it. Aubrey was going to be our child. She was the one we had been waiting for!

Aubrey came the next day and wasn't what I had imagined her to be. I had taken off work to

 welcome her into our home, and I waited several hours for her to arrive. In the meantime, I had studied my scriptures, prayed, and made sure the guest bedroom was ready. I cleaned out the closet to make room for all of her belongings.

A little after twelve, she arrived. She was tall for her age, a little dirty, and had extremely thin, curly, lice-infested, brown hair. She was nervous and talked a lot. She also hadn't come with anything but the clothes on her back. Bewildered, I made plans with Alan to take her shopping after he got home.

I was surprised how Alan immediately took to his role of being a father. After putting Aubrey to bed her first night, Alan commented on how his fears about loving a child not biologically his had vanished as soon as he saw Aubrey. We both instantly felt like she was meant to be our baby.

Those feelings were magnified as we got to know Aubrey. She definitely could be our biological daughter. Like Alan, she carried on the tradition of being smart for her age, witty, and craved learning. She was also outgoing, funny, and competitive—something we learned as she dominated us the first night in *Sorry*, the board game.

Aubrey was excited to have the freedoms we allowed her. She played in the basement, ate as much as she wanted at mealtimes, and picked the movies we watched. It was obvious she hadn't had many opportunities to be a kid.

Her worker, Sara, was great. She stopped by to check on Aubrey every month. She invested her time into Aubrey, made sure she was well, and was getting the help she needed from us as her foster parents and those in the community. Aubrey and I developed a beautifully close relationship and I felt blessed to have Sara's support as we loved and parented this incredible little girl.

Many people in our circle of family and friends extended unconditional love and acceptance towards Aubrey. Seasons changed, school let out, and summertime brought me more time with her. I finally was able to attend playdates with other women from church. It was something I hadn't dared do before, although I had been invited. It was at one playdate that summer that our lives changed again.

CHAPTER 5

Aunna

I have always had a love for literature, so I naturally chose to major in English in college. However, I knew that wasn't an ideal career choice. I needed to choose something in which I could easily obtain employment. I needed to support myself, so in my junior year, I switched to Elementary Education. It wasn't what I really wanted to do, but something that I sort of fell into. My older sister had majored in music education and I wondered if I could become an educator too. I was good with kids. Similarly, I had gained a love for teaching while serving as a missionary in Sydney, Australia; therefore, I felt good about this career choice.

One class, that education majors are required to take, is called Behavior Management. In this course, teachers are taught methods to help run their classrooms.

Positive and negative management techniques are studied and researched. The most common type of behavior management structure is a reward system. Children collect stickers, pom-poms, coupons, or money to earn the reward they desire. In order to collect, the child must act in accordance to a set of rules. During this new period of parenting, I began to see the benefits of choosing to become a teacher. I used those things I had studied and used to run my classroom, in my home.

A few weeks into summer break, Aubrey and I were at our usual Tuesday playgroup at the park. As I was talking with a friend, sharing her picnic blanket, I received another placement call. My heart felt as though it had skipped a beat. I thought, "Surely I'm not receiving another call already!" It was June—five months since our first placement. I had scarcely gotten to know Aubrey and now the State was going to ask me to take another child. I stepped away, towards the baseball field that ran alongside the playground and hesitantly answered the phone.

Aunna was in a foster home in a neighboring county. Her case was moving to the Louisville, Jefferson County Court System. In addition to this, her current foster home was deciding to close. This meant the foster parents were not taking in foster children any longer. She needed a home in Louisville, and Alan and I were being probed to take another five-year-old girl. I asked to call the placement worker back in a few minutes with my answer.

While sitting on the bleachers, I called Alan. He had taken the responsibility at church over the Young Men's youth group and it just so happened it was Boy Scout Camp that week. His phone went straight to voicemail, which only meant one thing: No signal. Alan had made me save the phone number to the main office at the camp in case of an emergency. I used it. A nice man picked up and said he would track Alan down and have him call me back as soon as possible. I waited.

About five minutes later my phone buzzed with the main office number of the camp. Whew! I inhaled and shared all that I was told about the little girl who needed a home. We again prayed and that same familiar burning in our hearts filled us with joy and peace. We knew this was another child that we had been waiting for. I called the placement worker and coordinated the process of meeting up with the current foster family to pick up Aunna.

We met at a McDonalds in Jeffersontown, a suburb of Louisville, a few days later. She was different than Aubrey—the opposite. Aunna was short for her age with straight blonde hair and green eyes. She looked like she had been malnourished at some point in her life. She was as skinny as a rail—wearing size 3T clothes. Aunna had lots of worries: Would I wash her clothes? Would there be food to eat? Would she like Aubrey? Would she have to share a room? Would she be moving very far? Would she be going to a new preschool? I answered each question with patience, which seemed to calm her anxieties.

Aunna also had lots of possessions, which immediately made Aubrey jealous. We unloaded several boxes of clothes and a bicycle the family had handed down to Aunna from one of their older daughters.

Aubrey had not come with anything and Aunna seemed to have the whole world packed up. Aubrey explained about our family, albeit defensively, to Aunna on the car ride home. Alan and I were *her* mom and *her* dad. Aunna seemed too anxious to comprehend the territorial remark. Yet, Alan and I laughed as we listened to their conversation in the back seat. Aubrey had, for the first time, called us mom and dad. I couldn't help smiling at Alan. Our family was growing.

We spent the rest of that year getting to know one another and growing together. Remembering my educational studies, I implemented a behavior rewards system to help both girls adjust. Each girl earned pom-poms on a chart and when the chart was full, they could earn a toy they liked. I always placed the toy on the fireplace mantle as a gentle reminder of what they were working for. This system helped the girls learn what was expected of them and conditioned their behaviors quickly, especially their jealousy for one another. I had to coach both of them on how to be a sister. I had to teach them about kindness and sharing, even sharing time with Alan and I.

When complaints about one another arose, I took the opportunity to remind them of how blessed they were to be with us. The Lord was mindful of both of them and their needs were being met. Both had questions about the future. Frequently I would remind them that only two things could happen: They would either stay with us, or go back to their birth families if it became safe. Both girls seemed at peace with either outcome. I perceived they understood: Staying meant having their needs met and being with people who reciprocated love for them. Leaving meant losing their peace of mind about their needs, yet they could keep the birth family each child loved dearly. Both situations had pros and cons.

Both girls had been taken from their birth families and they comforted one another in their moments of heartache. Regularly, I caught them embracing one another, with tears in their eyes, sharing how much they missed their birth families. At night I would hear them whispering in their bunkbed. They would reminisce about going fishing, camping, and swimming with their birth mothers. However, they would also discuss the negative memories too. Drugs and neglect were common factors. They both knew what it felt like to be hungry, tired, and cold. They knew what homelessness felt like and the unpredictability of the adults around them. Overhearing both girls realize they shared similar life challenges was striking. I learned many things about their past listening to those conversations, and it was eye-opening to witness how much they aided each other in healing.

Almost a year passed before our family was tested. We had become so normal—the four of us. It was hard to imagine a time without Aubrey and Aunna. They were such wonderful, obedient, little girls. It wasn't easy to picture that they had come from brokenness.

Aubrey and Aunna had started Kindergarten and I was blessed to be able to enroll them at the same school where I taught third grade. They did well in school, but sometimes it was hard to concentrate when they worried about their future. To help them cope with these worries, they were able to talk to an in-school therapist.

One night, in mid-May I received a phone call from the girl's therapist. She had never called me before, always preferring to speak to me at work. It was 6:30 at night and I was getting dinner cleaned up. "Katina," the woman began desperately, "what is the first name of Aubrey's birth mother?"

"Jody," I responded, "why?"

"Then I have some terrible news." She went on explaining what she had heard on the television news broadcast that evening. Aubrey's mother had overdosed on opiates and was found hours later in an abandoned house in downtown Louisville. I immediately called Sara to confirm this report. Sara hadn't heard from Jody in over 24 hours, but quickly got in touch with authorities to confirm the story. Sara said she would adjust her schedule the following day so she could come and break the news to Aubrey.

I knew this was going to crush her. She hadn't seen her birth mother in over a year, but she still loved her. Aubrey's love for her birth mother taught me that no matter how terrible we think someone is, we can still forgive, and we can still love that person. I loved Aubrey's birth mother because I saw how much Aubrey loved her.

Sara came to our house the following evening after school. Aubrey sat next to me on the couch while Sara spoke. Tears welled up in Aubrey's eyes; she stared almost blankly into the fireplace. I placed my hand on her back to comfort her. Like breaking glass, her heart was visibly shattered and she collapsed into a crying heap on my lap. I uncomfortably watched her grieve knowing there was nothing I could do.

I loved this girl. She was smart, talented, beautiful, yet her life was hard. She had endured much neglect and abuse. I grieved with Aubrey. I wanted to take away all her hurts—rewrite her life. I wanted to protect her from all she had suffered. Yet, I sat powerless to remove her pain.

Once Aubrey had calmed, asked all her questions, and Sara had left, we talked awhile about her mother. Her biggest regret was not being able to be there for Jody. Aubrey had witnessed her mother passed out from drugs before. In her young age, she had cared for her mother and nursed her back to health in those frightening moments. She almost blamed herself for not being there to wake Jody during an episode. I reminded her about the Spirit World, or heaven, and how I believed her mother could learn and grow, far away from the temptations and evil of this world. Jody would have the opportunity to repent.

While her birth mother's passing devastated Aubrey, she carried her grief with grace. She had a great love for the Savior, Jesus Christ. She had come to know Him through the scripture stories we had taught her. We discussed the temple and how, when she turned twelve, she could perform saving ordinances (such as baptism) for those who had passed. Her birth mother would have the chance to accept His Gospel in the Spirit World. I told her how Heavenly Father loves all of his children and would not punish Jody for ignorance. She had not known His commandments; therefore, He would be merciful to her.

Aubrey looked at me that evening and said through teary eyes, "Mom, I'm going to be the best I can be. I'm going to take my mom's name to the temple when I'm twelve and get her baptism done." Aubrey had learned about the Savior, the power of the Atonement, and the blessings of the temple only recently. Yet, she displayed great faith and understanding of God's plan in her statement. I held her tightly and we both cried.

CHAPTER 6

Rae

Tragedy seems most often associated with numerous casualties and catastrophes, like earthquakes, tsunamis, and terrorist attacks. Horrific things have happened in this world. Seeing children exposed to inappropriate things or ideas, and especially having to understand death at such a young age is heartbreaking. Here in lies the true tragedy: a culture where drugs, sex, and violence are the norm. How much heartache Aubrey truly endured? I will never know. She would often ask, "If I could have been there for my mom, would this have happened?"

Aubrey and I attended a private viewing of her mother at the funeral home. She was silent throughout the entire visit. I watched her closely, waiting for her to need my loving support. She picked a flower from her birth mother's casket and carried it between her fingers.

After some time, I lovingly put my arms around her and asked how she was feeling. Through teary eyes she said, "I know nothing can hurt her now." After several minutes of her watching the casket, we turned to leave. Our conversation on our way out turned to how the Savior loves her birth mother. I reminded her of the Spirit World and how Jody was learning of Him there. I wondered what else I could say to Aubrey to comfort her. Then I felt the Holy Ghost touch my heart.

The veil between the spirits of our ancestors and those alive on earth is very thin. There have been times in my life that I have called upon my Heavenly Father for comfort and He has answered my prayer through a relative, or someone from beyond the grave. For instance, I have always had a fear of flying. First, because I can't fathom my feet being so far off the ground, and second, I get extremely motion sick.

I remember when I was called to serve a mission for the church. I was being sent to Sydney, Australia for eighteen months. I had to attend a three-week training at the Missionary Training Center in Provo, Utah beforehand. My first time on a plane took me from Lexington, Kentucky to Cincinnati, Ohio. After a small 30-minute layover, I would travel to Salt Lake City, Utah where my cousin would pick me up. I said goodbye to my parents in the airport lobby and walked with faith that the Lord would watch over me on my journey. I boarded the plane and found my seat. Feeling my heart start to rise into my throat with panic, I again said a prayer that the Lord would protect me. I asked Him to keep me safe and pleaded with Him to help me not become sick. From beyond the veil, I heard the words of my grandpa Hobert, "I'm here doll," something he had always called his granddaughters. My heart burst with joy that my beloved grandfather was sent to comfort me in my time of need.

When I spoke to my daughter Aubrey, I relayed this experience to her and then felt impressed to share more. Being filled with the peace of the Spirit, I knew what her birth mother wanted Aubrey to know. I felt the Spirit impress upon my mind the exact words needed to comfort her. I told Aubrey that her mom was glad she was safe and would want her to learn all she could in this life. I told her that her mother would be proud of the choices that she was making and the things she was being taught. I reminded her of the temple and the work Aubrey could do for Jody there. She nodded and I held her for a minute outside the car. She was going to be okay, and I told her Jody would watch over her as she grew. Her mother was free from the pain of this world. Aubrey nodded and I knew that the things I said were enough. It was what Jody had wanted to tell Aubrey. We silently drove home and were both left to ponder on the words in which the Holy Spirit had communicated to my heart and mind. I was awestruck at how mindful the Lord was of us in that moment. I had been given a sacred opportunity to carry a message to my daughter.

Over time, with help from Sara, therapists, family,

and friends, Aubrey's pain eased and turned into hope. She hoped for better, happier days and was able to move past her grief. She graduated from therapy and was excited to be adopted.

January 10, 2017, almost two years since she came to live with us, we adopted Aubrey Kate Alami. We finally had our baby girl. On February 4, 2017 we took our daughter to the Louisville, Kentucky Temple to be sealed; we were pronounced a family for time and all eternity—one of the special blessings preformed for families in the temple. We weren't simply a family until death. Now my daughter was going to be mine forever. We rejoiced at the thought!

With Aubrey adopted, we eagerly turned our focus on Aunna. Her case was moving toward adoption and we wanted more children to expand our family. This thought prompted us to request another foster placement: a younger child, a boy perhaps. We called our caseworker, Holly, to ask that she open another spot in our home. She delightfully agreed.

✳✳✳

I was folding the laundry on a Monday afternoon two weeks later. The number for the Cabinet for Health and Family Services popped up on my phone. Gasp! It took us months to get our first placement. I felt like I should have a window of time to get used to the idea that we legally had one child. I didn't expect a phone call *that* fast! My heart thumped in my chest. Again, I was going to have to feel for the warmth of the Holy Spirit to guide me as I quickly made a decision for our family.

Living a life so that the Spirit can be a constant companion may sound easy, but is hard in practice. Reading scriptures, praying, and trying to keep all of God's commandments each day helps ensure that I continue to feel His presence. I made sure I was checking in with the Lord regularly to be able to rely on His Spirit for guidance. I had to lay down everything that once was precious to me: fashion, celebrity gossip, and shopping were a few things I had idolized. Laying aside the immature pleasures of youth was something that I decided to do a few years into marriage. I decided one night, as I prayed to Heavenly Father, to be better because I knew better. Material possessions or idolatry are not what bring true joy and happiness. I knew the Lord could change me if I let go of the cares of the world and live like He would have me live.

Learning that life lesson helped prepare me to become the mother I needed to be for my children. It helped me to understand the importance of living a Christ centered life; to put off the world, so that I could be worthy to have His Spirit guide me as I needed Him to do again now.

"Hello, this is Katina," my voice anxiously answered. I was informed that a nine-month-old girl was in kinship care, foster care with a relative, and her caregiver was no longer able to care for her due to health reasons. Her name was Emma Rae.

I felt it—that familiar burn within my chest. My

thoughts raced with excitement. A baby! She was what I had wished and prayed for! I quickly asked to talk to my husband and I would call the placement worker right back. I called Alan at work and we again prayed over the phone. Undeniably, we felt she was chosen to be ours. I called to accept the placement and started making preparations for a baby in our home. I started putting things out of reach, covering plugs, and arranging furniture around to accommodate a crib.

What happened next was no coincidence. It was the intervention and handiwork of God our Heavenly Father. Neil A. Maxwell, a latter-day apostle, once said, "None of us ever fully utilizes the people-opportunities allocated to us within our circles of friendship. You and I may call these intersectings 'coincidence.' This word is understandable for mortals to use, but *coincidence* is not an appropriate word to describe the workings of an omniscient God. He does not do things by 'coincidence' but instead by 'divine design.'"[11] Aubrey's former caseworker, Sara, called me within a few hours of accepting Emma Rae for placement.

I hadn't spoken with Sara since Aubrey's case had moved to adoptions and a new caseworker from that department was assigned to us. Sara excitedly informed me that she was the caseworker for Emma Rae. She was thrilled to be working with us again. We had developed a great relationship because of Aubrey and I knew Sara

---

[11] Neal A. Maxwell. *Brim with Joy*. Brigham Young University devotional address. 23 January 1996. p2. https://speeches.byu.edu/talks/neal-a-maxwell/brim-joy/

was going to do what was best for Rae.

Alan and I chose to call Emma Rae by her middle name. We thought it was cute and nicknamed her Rae-Rae. She was going to be someone special. I could feel it.

Sara disclosed to me what the placement worker had not: Rae was part of a sibling group. Sara had dealt with this case off and on for four years. Rae had three older brothers who were living with an aunt in west Louisville. She had been working with the birth parents, but they weren't making any changes in their behaviors. And more news, the judge they were assigned to in District Three was known for giving birth parents too many chances; therefore, the process of permanency and stability for the children was prolonged unnecessarily. It put a great strain on the children and the foster families involved. I knew the Lord wanted Rae in my home, so I had faith that no matter the bumps along the way, Rae was meant to be with me.

I arranged to pick her up at her Great Aunt Barbara's house. Alan and I climbed the stairs to the apartment over the garage and we knocked on the door. Sissy, the name Barbara preferred to be called, quickly invited us in. There in the middle of the living room floor was the cutest baby girl! She had strawberry blonde hair and bright blue eyes. She was a little chunky and stared at me confused. Not wanting to scare her, I smiled and kept my distance as Sissy explained her routine to us.

Sissy had taken great care of Rae. She gave us boxes of clothes, toys, books, shoes, and a crib to boot! Sissy obviously loved Rae. She had provided well for her, and desired to have Rae take everything with her that belonged to her.

It never occurred to me in that minute of happiness and lifelong dreams coming true, that someone else could be in so much sorrow. Sissy kept her warm smile on her face as we talked. I knew it must be hard on her, but the magnitude of what she was doing was lost on me. I didn't empathize with her pain because I was swallowed up in the joy of having Rae. I had never experienced loving a person so immensely and losing them. I had sympathy for Sissy, but I remembered that if she had not become sick and nearly died with pneumonia, I wouldn't be standing in her living room about to be the foster mother of the most beautiful baby girl in the world.

We loaded up the minivan and I allowed Sissy to buckle Rae into her car seat. She said goodbye and we left so Sara could help Sissy cope with the situation. Rae cried a little on the way home, but with every cry came also a laugh. Aubrey and Aunna were making silly faces at her in the backseat.

It was dark by the time we arrived home. We quickly bathed and dressed Rae for bed; yet, I again couldn't recognize the feelings of bereavement that were unveiling before me. Rae was fussy, tired, lost, but most noticeably, terrified.

CHAPTER 7

The Season of Rae

Rae was such a good baby. She grew attached to us quickly, which enabled her to overcome the trauma she had already experienced in her nine months of life. She was hospitalized at birth for opiates in her system and then taken from the only caregiver she had ever known. Yet, Rae had so many people to love her now: a mom, dad, two sisters, and our extended family. I continued to meet up with Sissy often so she could continue to watch Rae grow. I wasn't required to allow Sissy these visits, but I recognized the love Sissy had for Rae. We all cherished this precious baby girl.

My life changed when Rae came. With the responsibility of three kids to care for, I quit teaching and focused on being a stay-at-home mom. I felt like I was in a dream. I finally had the life that I wanted. I felt the joy that I had wished and prayed I would be given—

the opportunity to raise a
baby. Rae was healing me
as I put all of my focus on
being her mom while
Aubrey and Aunna were at
school; Rae helped Alan
grow into another role of
fatherhood as he fed and
played with her every
morning while the rest of
us slept.

Rae quickly associated the words, "ma·ma" and, "da·
da" with actual people—Alan and I. She was making
connections and thriving more than doctors thought she
might. We ventured out to playdates with friends. She
bonded quickly to many close to us. She was growing in
more ways than one.

In a short time, I had become so focused on my
growing family that I had forgotten about the emotional
baggage that lingered behind Rae. Two weeks after Rae
came to us, Sara called to inform me that Rae's three
older brothers—Robert, Jordan, and Camden—needed a
home. We casually discussed a few options for the boys
as they entered care. Sara believed we should not take all
three boys. The older two had serious difficulties that
needed to be addressed, which meant they would not be
a good fit for our home. However, she voiced the
potential benefits of placing Rae's two·year·old brother,

Camden, with us. Sara had previously mentioned his challenging behaviors, but I had seen the changes that the gospel had made in the lives of Aubrey and Aunna. I did not feel restrained by the Spirit, and without consulting Alan, I immediately said, "Yes!"

I called Alan as he drove home from work to confess to him that I had agreed to take Rae's brother if Sara's supervisor approved it. I explained to him how I felt like Camden was another one of those kids that we were meant to parent. The familiar burning in my heart from the Holy Spirit was present as I told him about the idea. I was learning how to trust that feeling. It had never betrayed me. Alan agreed that if we were given the opportunity, we would take Camden.

In the State of Kentucky there is a law that siblings must stay together where possible. As soon as Sara had brought the idea of Camden coming to live with us to her supervisor, it was immediately dismissed. Her supervisor wasn't going to separate the boys. I understood her concerns with separation, but that decision brought about feelings of doubt in myself. Had I actually had an impression from the Lord that Camden was meant to be in our family? Why did I feel that familiar warm feeling from the Spirit if he wasn't coming? I questioned the Lord, but I decided to be patient and wait on Him to help me understand. I continued to apply my faith in Him.

Sara called the next day informing me of the placement decision. The boys were placed in a therapeutic foster home the following day. Due to serious behaviors, the boys needed a therapeutic home with a couple trained in administering emotional and behavioral interventions. Alan and I were not yet certified to accept children with these specific needs, nor did we feel adequately equipped to handle them.

Sara also revealed that the birth mother was pregnant again. Knowing that the birth mother was still using drugs, Sara was being proactive in her foster placement search. Alan and I were the preferred home, since we had Rae in our care. I casually agreed to the idea. The child would be due in seven months, and I was sure Alan and I could be ready for another by that time.

The final thing Sara and I discussed on this call was parent and sibling visitation. We were being court ordered to begin both. In order to keep this as simple as possible, we met at a Necco office, a private foster care agency, to do both of these visits at the same time. I first saw Robert, Jordan, and Camden during our initial parent visit. The boys' foster mom was waiting in the playroom. I quickly went up to introduce myself. If these kids were going to need to visit every week, or would be adopted, I needed to have a good relationship with their caregiver or potential adoptive parent. She pointed out the boys by name. In that moment I remembered the feelings I had for little Camden. I desired to have this little boy, but knew that other plans were being put in place that kept me from having him.

We waited nervously for the birth mother to

arrive. Most people in these situations can be snobbish. Birth parents can be prideful and resentful towards foster parents, and some foster parents have been known to reciprocate or initiate those feelings first. I was anxious about seeing this birth mother, so I called my mom to help ease my fear.

My mother was sympathetic towards me. I loved Rae. It was frustrating to share her with someone who had hurt her. Rae didn't know her brothers or her birth parents, and I was worried to leave her with them for a visit. My mother paused and was quiet for a moment, listening to me vent. When I allowed her to speak, her tone was soft and understanding. She warned me to be kind, meek, and humble when I met their birth mother. I felt the burning of the Holy Spirit in my heart confirm her words. I did not need to act resentful towards their birth mother. The words from the Spirit entered my mind, "She is one of Heavenly Father's children, and He loves her too." I could not have prepared myself for visitation without that reminder.

After hanging up, I turned my attention to the boys, their behaviors, and how they adored their baby sister Rae. I tried to remember to be kind and meek regardless of my first impressions. However, this birth mother wasn't what I expected her to be. I smiled at her when she walked in; she returned my smile, was pleasant to talk to, and greeted me with courtesy. I told her about Rae and how she was growing. This mother generously appreciated the update. Soon I was asked to leave and let them have their one hour of time together.

I had managed to be kind, show love, and compassion in our short dialog. I was proud of myself that I had accomplished that. Knowing her history of drug abuse, neglect, and violence towards the children, I had managed to lay aside the negative for a moment and focus on the positive: She is a child of God. That was easy compared to what happened next.

It is tremendously distressing to have to leave a child you love with someone who has hurt them. Each visit I was required to place Rae in her birth mother's arms and walk away. I could be kind, but I didn't trust the woman who held her. Hearing Rae's cries behind me as I stepped out each week was excruciating. I never looked back. I couldn't. I didn't want to see her teary face watching me as I betrayed her trust. It was too painful. I wanted to stay near her, yet I kept my head up and walked out the door; I was required to follow the judge's court order. My feelings did not matter. I was just the foster parent.

It was torture to be separated from her during those visits. I cried in my car worrying about her as she cried inside. Nonetheless, I would return exactly an hour later to a baby girl who was happy to see my familiar face. She would reach for my arms and I would happily pick her up and hold her tight. I wiped the tears from her face. It was a relief to hold her again.

Several weeks went by and the birth mother refused to show up for visits, so the Necco office informed me they were canceled if I was not notified within a half-hour before each appointment. The next time the birth mother (and the father for once) actually decided to show up, I spoke with the boys' foster mom about my concerns. It was unfair to these kids. Why were the parents acting this way: Sometimes caring to see them, other times not? Their case looked as though it would be heading towards adoptions quickly. I asked the boys' foster mother if she was a concurrent planning home and was ready to adopt these little ones so they could stay together. She avoided my question. It seemed odd at the time, but with a few kids to gather and buckle up, I didn't have time to dwell on it.

After six months of non-compliance or when parents refuse to show up for their visits for ninety days, the Cabinet makes note and begins the process of petitioning the court for permanency, in other words, adoption. Sara petitioned the court a week later and then went on maternity leave. She was pregnant and due soon. Her replacement, Rachel, was kind and I liked her. She really tried to do her job and stick to the rule of law. I appreciated that in her; especially as the birth parents were not keeping their court orders. She saw that an adoption was likely going to happen in this case, but would need to convince the judge to process the adoption petition in the next hearing.

***

Cold weather subsided and spring came in full-bloom. Rae and I began to spend more time outdoors. Rae loved going to the zoo and riding in the stroller. She loved looking at the gorillas, but only from a distance—away from the glass enclosure. She shook from fear when she saw them, yet they captivated her. We also spent many hours in the park on her favorite swing. We met up with Sissy and had picnic lunches while we talked about Rae's future. Alan and I wanted to adopt her. Sissy wanted that for Rae too. She was overjoyed that Alan and I would allow her to be part of Rae's life.

April came, and we started to prepare Rae's big, one-year birthday celebration. I couldn't believe Rae was twelve months old. I had already missed so much of her life. I tried to make it the best birthday party ever. We decorated a room I booked from the church building and invited family, friends, and some appropriate birth family. We were all glad this little girl was born into our lives. She certainly had touched so many people in such a short amount of time. Rae enjoyed seeing many familiar faces. She wore a pink and gold glittered tutu that I had made for her party. She smiled brightly from all the attention. She was overjoyed at the opportunity to dive into her birthday cake with the freedom to make a mess!

At home that night, I put Rae's banner, tutu dress, and cake topper in her memory box. One birthday down! I couldn't wait to watch her grow into another! My girls were my whole world. I would give almost anything and everything for them.

May 10, 2017 started as a beautiful day. My best friend Shayla and I decided to spend the morning at the zoo. Like Rae, her eighteen-month-old little boy, George, loved the animals. It was warmer than it should have been and I had stripped Rae and myself out of our jackets down to our t-shirts. We stopped to look at the giraffes, elephants, and zebras. Both children gawked at the lions and gorillas. It was fun to see their faces as we strolled around the park showing them unique creatures. We rested and picnicked at a pavilion after a few hours of walking. Noticing how the sun and exercise had made us tired, we decided it was time to head back home for a needed afternoon nap.

I had scarcely been home five minutes when the phone rang with Rachel's number. I answered, thinking I could quickly see what she needed before I put Rae down to sleep. "Katina," she sounded tense, "I have something to tell you; the boys foster home closed and I am being asked to find another home for them."

"Oh no!" I responded. I was upset for the boys. I wondered if this had anything to do with the conversation I had with their foster mom a few weeks before—about needing to adopt them. They were being passed around like a mess someone didn't want to clean up. They already had to leave their birth parents, move in with an aunt, move to their grandpa's house, then moved to another aunt, placed in foster care, and now were being shuffled again. All of these moves happened within a year's time. I asked Rachel to let me know what happens, and thanked her for the information.

"I don't think you understand," she said more nervous than before, "when I look for a placement for the boys, I have to include Rae in my search."

"What do you mean?" I anxiously asked. My heart began loudly thumping inside my chest.

"I am going to have to place Rae with her brothers."

Silence. I couldn't say a word. I forgot how to talk. I was unsure of how many seconds had passed before Rachel broke the silence. "Are you okay?" she finally asked. I was speechless. I was *not* okay. I made an inaudible sound into the phone. "I will call you later, but the boys have to move by Wednesday," she finished and hung up.

CHAPTER 8

Not My Will, but Thine

I didn't even try to say goodbye. My legs collapsed and I sobbed into my hands. Tears streamed down my cheeks and created little puddles in my palms. Rae crawled over concerned about my wellbeing. She put her little hand on my cheek to comfort me and lifted my head. The agony on my face must have concerned her because she began to cry too. I lifted her up in my arms and held her tightly. My sobs turned into wailing and I held her even more tightly. "No, no, no!" I repeated over and over between moans. I couldn't accept this reality.

How could they take her from me? What could be done? How could God do this to me? She was *my* baby. Her birth mother hadn't bothered to show up for weeks to see her. I was giving this precious girl everything unconditionally, including keeping a relationship with Sissy—something I didn't have to do. I had to stop this. There wasn't any mother out there who would love Rae the way that I did. I was sure of it.

I can't recall how many minutes I sat weeping over my baby. I tried to pull myself together. Wiping my tears on the back of my hand, I gave Rae one last squeeze and warmed a bottle of milk for her. I laid her down a little late for her nap, but I was ready to pick up my courage and fight for this little girl. I called Alan.

Shocked at the news, he frantically began searching online, calling our caseworker Holly, and seeking out a loophole in the law that would allow us to keep Rae. While he researched, I called Sissy. She needed to know what they were trying to do to our baby girl. It was the most dreadful conversation I have ever had with someone.

Sissy and I felt betrayed by the State. Sissy had trusted Sara to find a good home for Rae when she left kinship care; but Sara wasn't around this time. She was still on maternity leave. Rachel and her supervisor were left to decide what was best for the kids on Sara's caseload. The timeline on paper showed I couldn't have become very attached to Rae, because she had only lived with us three months. Someone who had been in my home daily would have seen otherwise. Sissy begged me to organize a plan to stop this. I told her Alan was working on something, but I didn't know what the outcome would be.

After speaking with both Alan and Sissy, I ran to my bedroom and threw myself to my knees to pray. I began pouring out my heart to my Heavenly Father. He had the power to stop this from happening. He could soften their hearts. He could take away my hurt. He could save my daughter Rae. She was mine. I had felt it.

I pleaded with Him to intervene. I had been taught that everything could be made right through the Atonement of Jesus Christ, so I begged the Lord to make this right. He had led me this far by His Spirit. He had guided me to take each of these girls. Why had He done this; why had He been so careful to instruct me which children to choose if I couldn't keep them all? I prayed for understanding and to find a way to keep Rae.

Holly couldn't help. The only advice she could give us was to contact the ombudsman's office and plead our case. She also advised us to contact the children's guardian-ad-litem, let her know our feelings, and see if she would intervene. The following letter was sent to both parties:

> My name is Katina Alami. My husband Alan and I are foster parents in Jefferson County. We currently have in our care a one-year-old baby named Emma Rae. A decision regarding her placement has been made that has us concerned, as we believe it is not within her best interest.
>
> On Wednesday of this past week, I received a call from the child's current social worker Rachel, who has taken over for the original worker, Sara, who is on maternity leave. In the call we were informed that the child's siblings are being moved to their sixth placement after being

removed from their birth mother's care, and that the new [home] has four placements available. As a result, the workers responsible and/or their supervisors had made the decision to remove Emma Rae from our home to be placed with her siblings as is normally recommended under the law.

We feel that this decision is inappropriate once all factors are considered in Emma Rae's situation. As a result, we reached out to Susan, who is Rachel's supervisor. After some discussion of our concerns, she agreed to discuss the placement decision with her supervisor, who's name I do not have. We followed up yesterday and the decision remained, after which we discussed additional concerns and Susan felt it reasonable to consider those things and reach out to her supervisor again expecting to follow up with me today (Friday 5/12/17). However, she called my husband back within only a few hours claiming that a final decision had been made regarding the placement of the child. I do not know if Susan herself made the decision, or if it was her supervisor, but I will outline some of the reasons why we feel it is not in the child's best interest.

Emma was originally placed in the care of family, Barbara, and was not with her three brothers. At just over 8 months Barbara felt her health was a challenge in raising the child and elected to have her placed in the foster system. My husband and I personally went to Barbara's home along with Sara, and picked up the child, who has been in our care since then. We established a relationship with Barbara and that side of Emma Rae's family, and have remained in contact on a continual basis which would be our long-term plan should she remain in our care.

In our discussions with Barbara, and based on the sibling visits I have attended, we were informed that the family felt it may be in the best interest of the child to keep her separated from her three brothers, especially assuming she remained in our home. However, we attended sibling visits as arranged. Outside of the occasional one-hour court appointed sibling visits, Emma Rae has never been with her brothers. She does not know them, and does not have a relationship with them, as when in Barbara's care, our understanding is that visitation was not done, it only began once in the care of the Cabinet of Kentucky. Each time Emma has been with her brothers, or had brief visits with her mother, she cries continuously until she is returned to us.

We feel that the decision being made is inappropriate. As explained before, this child does not have a relationship with her brothers, but has developed a great relationship with me, my husband, and our other two daughters. We already have a well-established relationship with the child's family and original caretakers, who even were present at her first birthday party along with us. Barbara and family have already expressed the strong desire for this child to remain in our home, and the desire that we would adopt her should the opportunity come (which we would).

Emma Rae's three brothers are now being moved to their third [foster] home. There are various factors resulting in the moves, some of which the original family placement has indicated to us, through Barbara, was difficulty in handling behaviors. The main reason this is of concern is because Emma is being removed from an already well-established home where she is being well cared for and loved, and has developed strong attachments, to be placed in a different home, not returned to her parents. If that home were to have a placement disruption, there is no way to predict that another home would be available to take all four children, and even if there were, you are creating multiple moves that could further negatively impact this child who would not be affected in such a way should she remain with us.

Emma Rae's mother is currently pregnant with another child to be delivered later this year. We have already agreed to accept that child into our home as we have Emma and would then have her sibling also. With the new placement, it has not been confirmed as to whether or not they would accept the fifth child, which, if they do not, would still result in a separation of siblings, which is the only reason being given for the placement change at this time. Emma Rae has an established relationship with our daughters as her siblings in our home. Therefore, there is no evidence to suggest the goal of this placement change will actually be achieved to an acceptable extent. There is also no current indication that the new foster placement would be willing to maintain a relationship with the biological family of the children as we have done with Barbara and others.

There are so many different possibilities, and issues that could come up that we feel it is unwise, unfair, and inappropriate to Emma Rae, to remove her from a loving home where she is well established for the sole purpose of being placed with blood siblings who she does not know, who do not know her, and who have only met briefly on rare occasion. Our family, her family, and former caretakers also have a developed relationship. It will be a disruption to this child's happy and safe life, simply for the possible chance of a positive result. Is it truly the wisest decision to act when there are so many unknown factors, in direct opposition to the already known and established positive condition of this child's life? My husband and I do not think so. Barbara has also contacted Susan to express her disagreement with this decision, even pleading to take the child back into her care rather than have this decision enacted (which unfortunately cannot be done due to health reasons).

In the court system, parents are often granted extension to the 22-month permanency rule on a subjective basis as the judge considers their individual situation. Similarly, we feel the most appropriate decision for Emma Rae to be reached in the same light, a subjective review of all factors related to her individual situation. We believe once this is done, it will be clear that the best thing for her is to remain in our care.

We are unsure of who ultimately has made this greatly impactful decision, but we feel it is the wrong decision and are requesting action on behalf of Emma Rae to prevent it from being enacted this upcoming Wednesday, May 17th... We love Emma Rae—my husband, my daughters, myself, her extended family, former caretakers (including Barbara), and others. We all sincerely want what we believe is best for her life and well-being.

Sincerely,
Alan and Katina Alami

We had hoped that someone would read this letter and sense the love and concern we had for Rae. The responses we received were less than hopeful. Alan spoke with the ombudsman office and they instructed us that there was nothing they could do. The decision remained with the Cabinet and the supervisor who reviewed the case. The same response came from the guardian-ad-litem; she would side with the Cabinet.

Alan and I were furious. Our baby girl was slipping away from us and those with the authority to stop it were refusing to exercise their power. I was angry with God. Why was He not exercising *His* power? Rae was supposed to be *my* daughter. Why had He given me the revelation if it was not meant to be? I was frustrated at the Lord and again begged Him in prayer to make this right. We needed a miracle; it was in His hands now.

The apostle John taught, that those who are sick or afflicted should, "call for the elders of the church; and let them pray over him."[12] Being in need of comfort and healing, I sought a blessing from Alan because he was an Elder in our church. I needed every power in Heaven and earth to be on my side. I knew the Lord loved Rae more perfectly than I did. I had faith He was listening to my cries. I needed to know, why was He staying his hand?[13] Alan miserably looked at the floor. He quietly said, "I can't do that. This involves me. I'm afraid I might say something contrary to the Lord's will just because I want

---

12 James 5:14

13 Daniel 4:35

it to be that way." I nodded and understood. We were both grieving. We were hurt. No matter how much we prayed to God for a miracle, it wasn't going to happen. It wasn't His plan for Rae to stay with us. We hugged and cried together. This was it; we were defeated. We were out of time, so we decided to make memorable the days we had left.

Sunday was Mother's Day. The worst one in my memory. The girls woke me up to a cooked breakfast in bed, balloons, and some pictures they drew on a card. I smiled and cried. I couldn't bear the thought of losing one of my babies on Mother's Day. We went to church and the response from friends was heartwarming. I was greeted by many friends with a hug and sympathy. They truly were saddened by what was happening to our family. Rae had touched so many people. Most who had spent time with her were smitten. This wasn't fair—to her or us.

After church we went home to spend time together as a family. We put Rae down for a nap and I retired to my bed for one as well. Before I laid my head down, my mother called. "Katina, I got a blessing today because I knew you wouldn't be able to get one before Rae left." My eyes welled up with tears. I hadn't spoken to my mother about my desire for a blessing, yet here she was being prompted by the Spirit to receive instruction from the Lord when I couldn't.

My mother was struggling. She had made a baby blanket for every grandbaby who came into our family.

She had recently decided to make one for Rae. She had carefully picked out the pastel African animal fabric and pink plaid backing. The time, work, and love she put into that blanket seemed to have been in vain. There had always been a risk that Rae would leave, but we never imagined a child would be forced to leave our home, except to be reunited with their birth parents.

I listened intently to my mother's words. She said the Lord wanted me to know a few things: First, the Lord was mindful of Alan and I. Second, there was a plan for Rae and it would not be frustrated. I was told to "be still"[14] and see the hand of the Lord. Third, "things will be better than [they were] before."[15]

I paused at the third thing my mother paraphrased. What was that supposed to mean? How could anything be better than having my Rae? I didn't want anything else. I was ready to give up all of my material possessions if it meant we could keep her! Alan was too.

I was confused and angry that God would not reveal more. I was distraught, yet I still hoped for the day that somehow this would be made right through Christ. I wished there were another way, but I gathered one thing: Rae was supposed to leave. Heavenly Father needed her to leave our home for some purpose that I did not yet understand. I wept as my mom tried to comfort me.

---

14 Spurlock, Janie. Personal Journal. 13 May 2017.

15 Spurlock, Janie. Personal Journal. 13 May 2017.

My mother conveyed how important it was that we had taught Rae the gospel. She believed the primary songs we had sung so many times would later be familiar to Rae. She would have the gospel of Jesus Christ and embrace it because of the things we taught her in the three months she had lived with us. This had been my biggest worry, and her words put me at ease. I wanted Rae to have the gospel of Jesus Christ. I wanted her to know her Savior. I wanted her to know she was a child of God.

I was grateful my mother had sought comfort through a blessing. It brought me some relief. We said goodbye. Then, I began to pray.

CHAPTER 9

The Trial of Faith

Praying was difficult. It was beyond difficult; it was agonizing. I could hardly speak through my tears. My thoughts about the will of God for Rae had changed; as a result, the words I prayed on her behalf, and ours, changed too. I didn't plead with the Lord to stop this tragedy. I prayed that He would help me through it. I prayed for Rae to be comforted and that God would watch over her wherever she went. I prayed that she would be loved, and remember the love that we felt for her. I prayed for strength to let her go.

Tuesday arrived and Rae and I spent the day playing, singing songs, and reading her favorite books, while Alan and the girls were at work or school. That afternoon Alan had managed to come home from work a few hours early. Rachel, the caseworker, had made an appointment for us to meet the foster mother who would take Rae. She hoped it would help our uneasiness about the transition.

Rae would be going to her new foster home the next day. I was curious to meet the woman who would be caring for my baby. We met at a Baptist church about a mile down the road that ran behind our house. I wondered how close this family lived to us, because this foster mother had chosen a meeting location nearby.

Michelle was a wonderful woman and very Christian, which I appreciated. Yet, I felt sorrow and some contempt as we talked. She had already taken Robert, Jordan, and Camden into her home and they had been there for a few days. She was waiting on Rae. I felt like a kid who didn't want to share. It wasn't Michelle's fault Rae was leaving, so I couldn't blame her for the poor decision of the State. I tried to be grateful that Michelle was willing to pacify Rae when the foster system had failed her.

I noticed Camden playing on the slides and I thought again about my revelation concerning him. How was he supposed to be mine when I wasn't even allowed to keep his sister? This was all very wrong. I sensed it. But I could do nothing about it. I had hope that "things would be better than they were before" and continued to have faith in God and His promises. I turned my focus on getting to know Michelle.

She seemed easy to talk to and trust. I related to her all of my concerns about this move. She understood and had compassion for us. She hugged me and we cried together as she shared how the Lord had instructed her to help a family of children. I appreciated her honesty and sharing her spiritual prompting with me. The Lord was orchestrating something that neither of us could see. She was being asked to be an instrument in the hands of God[16] to accomplish something, and that was all she knew.

I let Michelle hold Rae for a few minutes before we said goodbye. She would have time to bond with Rae tomorrow. Our family's time was running out. We left to pick Aubrey and Aunna up from school on our way home. Despite the desire to greedily keep her to myself, I allowed Alan and the girls to each spend time with Rae that evening. It was the opportunity I needed to start the dreaded task of packing. I barricaded myself in Rae's room. I didn't want my husband and children to see me so distraught. I spent two hours crying as I packed up her things. With each new bin a whole new wave of tears commenced. Her clothes, her toys, her pictures, all the memories and evidence that proved she was part of our family were vanishing. My faith in the Savior and His promises was all that gave me peace.

The thought would frequently come to my mind, "remember the words of your mother." It was hard to remember the Savior and His promises when all I wanted was *my* Rae. In that moment, I didn't care about anything else. In my grief, another thought came to

---

16 Alma 17:9

mind, "If you had walked in the days of Christ, you would have loved Him. You would have wanted to save him from persecution, spittings, whippings, His suffering in the garden, and most of all His crucifixion. You would have wanted to remove His pain, like His mother Mary. However, this would have frustrated God's plan and thwarted the salvation of mankind." We had been repeatedly taught in our training the mantra, "moves hurt kids." I wanted to protect Rae from the trauma of relocating to a new home and family. I wanted to keep her safe forever, but in doing this I would be thwarting the plan that God had for her. I had to step back and allow this happen—as did Mary—as did our Father in Heaven with His Son, Jesus Christ. Knowing all this didn't alleviate my affliction, but it helped me to have an eternal perspective; it lightened my burden as I began to see Rae the way Heavenly Father sees her. After all, she was *His* Rae.

I cuddled on Rae the rest of the evening. I read her a book, sang her a song, rocked her to sleep, placed her in bed, and watched her. I couldn't take my eyes off her. Every moment was precious to me. I wanted to soak up and remember as many as I could.

Alan snuck in behind me. He grabbed my hand and rubbed the back of it with his thumb. We watched Rae's chest rise and fall as she slept. This was it; no more bedtime routines. No more middle of the night check-ins to see if she was still breathing. No more good night stories, songs, or kisses; our last ones fleeting.

I felt Alan tug me towards the door. I didn't want to, but allowed myself to be pulled out of Rae's room. We paused outside in the hall. Alan pulled me into his chest and held me close. He knew how much I hurt. He hurt too.

Wednesday morning dawned and Rae was up an hour and thirty minutes before her usual 8am wakeup. I could tell she sensed something was happening. She was uneasy and would cry when she couldn't see me. We kept Aubrey and Aunna home from school. They needed to say their goodbyes too. We ate breakfast as a family, and played Rae's favorite games: boom (falling on her butt and shouting, "Boom!") and jumping in a pile of crumpled up junk mail. She loved the sale ads and coupons, and once per week, on Wednesday when they came in the mailbox, she would gather them in a pile, then jump, and scatter pages of the advertisements all over the floor. We read her favorite book, <u>Pete the Cat: I Love My White Shoes,</u> and sang her favorite songs, "I Am a Child of God" and "Families Can Be Together Forever."

Alan and I wept through the last song as we sang: "I have a [family] here on earth. They are so good to me. I want to share my life with them through all eternity."[17] We felt eternity was out of reach for us with Rae. I remembered again how I was taught that all could be made right through the Atonement of Jesus Christ. How

---

[17] Text: Ruth M. Gardner, 1927–1999. © 1980 IRI Music: Vanja Y. Watkins, b. 1938. © 1980 IRI https://www.churchofjesuschrist.org/music/library/hymns/families-can-be-together-forever?lang=eng&_r=1

was He going to make this right for me? For Rae? I still had faith He would, but veiled from His plan for our

lives, doubt lingered.

We loaded up Rae's boxes and crib in the minivan. Everything was gone—her spaces bare. We drove to the Neighborhood Place government office in Middletown, a suburb of Louisville. The ride was agony, but I could feel the peace of the Spirit. I deliberately tried to keep that Spirit close. I wanted to feel the joy that comes from it. I needed His warmth. I was drowning in emotion and I needed His strength to get through this.

We pulled up out back, parked, and transferred all of Rae's belongings into Rachel's vehicle. I held Rae. I squeezed her tightly as she looked around at all her things being moved from our car to the next. I pulled out a bottle. She pushed it away unable to eat, although it was her usual mealtime. Aubrey and Aunna clung to me as I held Rae. I wanted to press pause or freeze time. I wanted to stay stuck in that moment with my baby held tightly to my chest forever.

It was time. Rachel opened the back door of her mid-size SUV and I grudgingly placed Rae in the car seat. She screamed. Her little hands fought me as I shoved her down into an unfamiliar vehicle. I buckled her holding back my tears. She yelled all the louder, reaching her hands toward me. I gave her one last kiss, placed her bottle within her reach, and closed the door. I felt powerless, but had been given the strength from God to do what had been asked of me. Alan pulled me into his arms. In all our years of marriage, I have never seen him cry as profusely as he did when Rae left.

CHAPTER 10

Goodbye and Goodbye

Alan and I turned to our girls, Aubrey and Aunna. We hugged them tightly and ushered them into the minivan. We had to get away from this terrible scene. Being left to watch our Rae disappear was crushing. We drove down the road towards the mall to take the girls out to eat. We needed a distraction—something to lighten the mood. We quietly sobbed and held hands with one another in the car. Rachel's SUV stayed in front of us for a few stoplights and then made a left turn. "Goodbye Rae," I thought, "I love you." I turned around in my seat to watch the vehicle disappear completely from view.

I grasped Alan's hand tighter and we both commented on the peace we felt. I was reminded of the scripture, "I can do all things through Christ which strengtheneth me;"[18] we were forced to confront the truth of this witness in a way that is experienced by few. The Atonement of Christ was working for us. It was comforting us as we struggled to pick up the pieces of our broken hearts and move on. What would life look like without Rae? I had become a stay-at-home mom. I didn't have a job. What would I do when the girls went back to school? I would be alone. I pushed those feelings aside. I couldn't gauge that right now. I reminded myself to take things one day at a time.

We took the girls out for juicy hamburgers and fries. Aubrey and Aunna were both appreciative of the meal and getting to dine out, but it didn't change the effort it took for them—for all of us—to smile. I tried to explain the situation the best I could. Heavenly Father loves us and Rae, and He needed us to let her go. It was hard for them. They had the same questions I did. They wanted to know why, and I didn't have any answers for them; nothing but the assurance that the Lord had a plan and we had to trust in His wisdom. I am not sure how much they believed as Alan and I tried to explain.

We tried to have a good time and put all our attention on the girls and healing our family. We headed back home and played some games before bedtime. I checked my email as the girls got ready for bed, and my heart was touched.

Michelle and her husband, Octavio, had emailed us

---

18 Philippians 4:13

a quick note to tell us that Rae was safe, happy, and went to sleep right on time without a single pout. The next day they sent a picture of Rae eating dinner from the night before. She was smiling and happy. All I wanted for her was happiness, health, and a  sound mind. From the picture, she looked like all of those things. Michelle's home looked clean and well taken care of from the background, and Rae's two little teeth were poking out in a big grin as she stuffed her mouth full of food. I sighed and my heart was relieved. I could lay my head down to sleep at night with peace that, at least where she was, she was going to be okay.

Summer approached quickly and the girls were finishing up their last two weeks of school. I spent those several days engrossed in doing things for them. I attended field day at their school and tried to volunteer a little more in the classroom. I cleaned the house top to bottom and played hymns and spiritual music on the radio to help ease my loneliness and pain as I went about the day.

Breaking down in tears on the floor became a daily occurrence. I knew I had done what the Lord had asked of me. Yet, I still felt loss. Through the grief, I knew the Savior was present. I was feeling His succor, which only can be felt through the trial of faith. I loved Rae, and the blow of losing her was softened by the love of the Savior. He placed peaceful feelings into my heart and mind.

One afternoon I was mopping the floors, listening to a Christian radio station. A song came on I had never heard before. Listening to the lyrics made my eyes water and I stopped to have a tender moment with the Spirit. I was reminded how the trials of our lives can feel like a raging storm; however, the Lord allows us to endure that storm for a wise purpose. His trying of our faith can actually be a manifestation of His mercy.

I knew that this trial was a tender mercy[19] from the Lord. He needed me to grow in faith, and He had also provided me with promised blessings if I kept that faith. This trial was what he was using to refine me, yet it came at the cost of my precious Rae, and that bothered me.

Alan's boss at work showed us sympathy. She purchased us annual Kentucky Kingdom Theme Park passes to give our family something to do together. She hoped it would help us emotionally connect with one another and distract us from the hurt we were experiencing. I was moved by her kindness. It was exactly what we needed. Summer was in full swing and it was good to get out of the house. We went a few Saturdays with Alan in tow, but mostly the girls and I went while

---

[19] 1 Nephi 1:20

he worked. We soaked up the sun at the waterpark and enjoyed rides almost every day. Most importantly, we were smiling; we were healing.

It was hard to imagine life moving on when Rae left. Yet, life did continue on and appointments were kept. Aubrey and Aunna had a scheduled dentist appointment (June 12, 2017), so we took a time-out from our theme park thrills. The dental hygienist quickly ushered the girls back into the examination chairs and I called my mother to check-in with her while I waited. I wasn't on the phone more than two minutes when the door opened and Jordan walked into the office. Jordan turned to hold the door wide. My heart skipped a beat. Robert and Camden ran in next. Like in slow motion my eyes widened, my heart thumped loudly, and I became excited. I felt blood pumping in my ears. Michelle turned the corner pushing a single black stroller where *my* little Rae sat quietly. "I have to go mom," I quickly blurted, "Rae just walked into the dentist office!" I hushed my mother's confused huffs as I hung up on her.

Louisville has many dental offices, there's nearly one on every corner. I marveled at this coincidence. Michelle just so happened to bring the kids to the same practice, on the same day, at the same time as us. Was this coincidence or fate? Was this another mercy from the Lord?

Michelle seemed to become nervous when she saw me. She watched Rae anxiously as I approached them. Would Rae remember me? About a month had passed since our last goodbye. I knelt down at the stroller and asked Michelle if I could get her out. She nodded hesitantly. I unbuckled the strap and picked Rae up. Rae looked at me with those bright blue eyes. For a moment, I expected her to hug me, kiss me, or jump for joy. She quickly turned her head towards the toys in the waiting area and wiggled her way out of my arms to play with the Legos.

I was shocked; she didn't remember me? No. She had to remember me! I quickly sat on the floor beside her and called out her name, "Rae, Rae?"

"We call her Emma now because that is what our caseworker advised us to do," Michelle responded.

I stood up and leaned on the wall as I watched her play with her brothers. Rae had never gone by her first name before. Sissy had called her Boo when she lived with her. Alan and I thought the name Rae was cute and she seemed to like it too.

Michelle sat down in the chair next to me to fill out intake forms. I instinctively glanced over—if I were any other stranger, such an innocent glance would be meaningless. I couldn't help but notice the home address she had written down. A brief glimpse had revealed to me where *my* baby lived; it was only a few miles from our house! In that split second the words on that page seemed to have become permanently etched into my mind. Rae had not been far from us all along!

Aubrey and Aunna came back from their cleanings and were surprised to see their baby sister playing happily. I checked out with the receptionist, but stayed to watch Rae and let the girls visit. Rae didn't seem bothered at all that we were there. She kept playing, but glanced up to look at us every so often. I wondered if she felt betrayed when we sent her away. I wondered if she was content in Michelle and Octavio's family. Was her contentment the reason she wasn't reaching for me? Ultimately, she was happy. I was glad because that meant I could be happy.

After several minutes, I sensed that we were crowding the waiting area. I could tell Michelle was feeling overwhelmed by our presence. Reluctantly, I told the girls to say goodbye and ushered them toward the door. I crouched low beside Rae, planted a kiss on her cheek, and whispered, "I love you Rae." I know it was the peace of Christ that gave me the strength to get up and walk away from her again that day. This time, on a happier note.

CHAPTER 11

Healing

Aubrey, Aunna, and I enjoyed the rest of our summer. In between theme park outings we frequently had playdates with our friends Shayla and George. Coincidentally, to get to and from their apartment, it was necessary to drive by Michelle and Octavio's house. We passed their split-level almost once a week on the way to our playdate. Each time we passed their home my heart burst with anxiety. I wondered: Did Rae ever look out the window? Did she play in the yard? Was her room upstairs or down? It seemed foolish to me to have these questions. Yet, I thought about them every trip that took me in their direction. I couldn't resist slowing down a little to try and catch a glimpse of Rae, but I restrained myself from stopping. As much as I wished and longed in my heart to see her, I knew that the best thing for Rae was for me to keep my distance. I was pleased that Rae was doing well in her new foster home, and I couldn't have asked for more than Rae's happiness.

My life began to feel like a waiting room. Like waiting to see a doctor, I was waiting for the Lord to come out of a side door and call me back. I was waiting on the Lord to make things right. I was waiting on Rae to grow up. I wanted to see how her life turned out. I hoped for a future day when she would come back to me, but I wasn't holding out on it. I felt the Spirit's comfort daily and I continued to "be still." I was patiently waiting and watching for His promise of "things [to] be better than they were before."

As August approached, depression started to set in. August meant the girls were heading back to school and I would be alone during the day—again. I cherished the time I had with my daughters. Aubrey and Aunna had been a daily distraction for me. I was worried I would again begin feeling the emptiness that came from losing Rae.

As I dealt with the anxiety of looming solitude, it just so happened that Aunna received an adoption court date scheduled for the beginning of October. I eagerly distracted myself with preparations to add her to our forever family. I created her adoption announcements, planned celebratory events, and shopped for decorations for her special day. Beyond this, I found time to read books and complete craft projects. Still, I began to miss

Aubrey and Aunna; it was difficult for me to abruptly transition from having children around during the day to none at all. I thought about Rae more often during those lonely hours. I missed her and wondered if I would ever stop missing her.

Shayla and George came to visit a few weeks after school started back to ease some of my loneliness. During this visit, Shayla revealed she would be starting a new job and needed a sitter for George for a few hours each day. We agreed that perhaps he could help me not to feel so lonely. I happily accepted her offer.

The Lord knows what He is doing. He is a great and masterful designer. When I felt so lonely, He offered this: A chance to be with a child—to cuddle, care for, and nurture him. Shayla needed help, but so did I. George helped me process my grief; he didn't replace Rae—nothing ever could. Yet he helped me heal as I spent my energy focused on him and his needs during those hours the girls were at school.

I was grateful for the time I spent with George. We laughed and giggled as we played with his cars. We danced together to music and watched <u>How the Grinch Stole Christmas</u> on repeat. He kept me busy, and I appreciated the distraction. However, it was short lived.

Shayla was pregnant and welcomed George's sister Leslie into the world September 13, 2017. This meant that George was being watched by his grandparents during the day and I went back to being alone at home. I was happy for Shayla and knew she appreciated the support from family as she welcomed her new baby girl. However, without George to divert my attention, I was left again thinking and aching for Rae.

I desperately wanted more children to fill the void Rae had left. Alan and I were ready to move forward. We called Holly, our caseworker, to open two placements for our family. About a week after opening our home, we were called for a sibling group, a four-year-old boy and two-year-old girl. I called Alan and we prayed over the phone like every time before. The feeling that came from the Spirit was different this time. We had a good feeling, but it wasn't as powerful as Aubrey, Aunna, or Rae's placement confirmations. We reasoned that good feelings come from God, so it was probably okay with the Lord to accept these children. We called their worker and accepted placement. After court the following day, we were told the judge wouldn't sign the documents to place them in foster care. It was hard emotionally. I wasn't sure if I should be happy or sad for these children. But it wasn't my job to decide if these children required a foster home, so I didn't dwell on it.

On another occasion we were asked to take a group of three siblings (two boys and a girl). Again, Alan and I prayed over the phone and received a similar feeling from the Spirit: A good feeling, but not as powerful as the others. We continued in faith and accepted the siblings for placement. After three weeks of making preparations for them to come, a relative came forward at the last minute to care for them. We were trying, but our efforts seemed to be repeatedly foiled.

Sara came back from maternity leave and called me. She apologized for what happened in her absence. Seeming to understand how I was feeling, she sympathized with my heartache. She mentioned again how Rae's birth mother was pregnant and due in November. Michelle and Octavio were not eager to take the newborn baby girl. She asked if Alan and I would be willing to take her. I began to feel angry. How dare she offer me this baby! She could never replace her sister Rae!

Keeping my cool, I declined her offer. I wouldn't take any of Rae's siblings without Rae. Besides, the State could just as easily rip this baby out of my arms. I had to protect my heart.

After that conversation, Rae continued to weigh heavily on my mind, and I wondered why. I kept thinking about her baby sister preparing to enter this world. She was going to be born dependent to opiates just like Rae had been. I wanted to help, but I couldn't bring myself to take this baby without Rae as a package deal.

Sara called me again the next day. I was on the soccer field watching Aubrey practice. She expressed how horrible she felt about what had happened. She revealed that Michelle and Octavio were feeling overwhelmed with the children they had. This unborn baby girl would either have to be separated from her siblings or these siblings would have to move again. The easiest plan was for us to take the baby. Yet, my decision was the same—not without Rae.

I hung up and dialed Sissy's number. We had spoken every so often during the past few months. I kept her up to date with things from the State as I found them out. She had been able to see Rae at grandparent visits as the boys still had a healthy relationship with their maternal grandfather and Sissy drove him to those appointments. She likewise kept me informed about how Rae was doing and what she could tell about the children's progress.

I took a big breath and told her what Sara had been asking of me. I told her how I felt about it and what she thought I should do. I didn't want to get hurt. Not again. Sissy listened quietly, which was unusual for her nature. When I expressed all that I could, she responded, "Please take that baby. You deserve her. Think about it, she could be the key to having a relationship again with Rae." I was surprised. She knew how hard it was for me to move forward without Rae. Could this be the plan the Lord had?

I told Sissy I'd think about it. I went for a walk around the field. I needed to clear my head. I started to pray in my mind, "Heavenly Father," I pleaded, "I need thy guidance." I expressed to him all that was happening and my fear about taking this unborn baby. The sweet warmth of the Spirit followed as I paused my prayer to listen for the words of God to come to my mind.

"This child is yours," the words echoed clear in my head. I felt peace warm my heart and knew the words were from my Heavenly Father.

And then I heard the sweetest voice reply, "Mom, I'm coming."

I stopped and gazed up towards heaven. The sun was peeking behind a cloud, its rays bouncing off the tallest trees surrounding the field. Did I really just hear *her* voice?

Yes, the Spirit was witnessing to me that I had heard correctly. I was being called as this child's mother. Whatever the outcome of Rae, I had to take her sister. *She* had spoken to me.

Chapter 12

The Lord's Time

Alan listened silently as I described my spiritual experience to him that night. He didn't have much to say, but agreed that we would take the baby if Michelle and Octavio would not. They still were the preferred foster home. They could still choose to take her.

The next morning, I was anxious as I waited until nine o'clock to call Sara—which was when I knew she would be at her office. I told her, after discussing it with Alan, I had changed my mind. We would take the baby if she could not be placed with her siblings. In the middle of our conversation, I received a text message— from Michelle!

Michelle had always communicated through email. I was stunned that she was choosing to text me five months after I had given her my phone number, and at the exact moment I was reaching out to Sara about Rae's sister! Her text message read that her and Octavio were disrupting their placement. She needed to talk to me as soon as possible. My jaw dropped. Not wanting to alarm Sara, I stumbled through the rest of our conversation. I didn't mention what was happening because Michelle and Octavio needed to be the ones to tell Sara their decision.

I dialed the number hurriedly. I was eager to find out more. "Hello. Michelle?"

"Hold on a second," she begged. I heard her shuffle some kids in the background. A minute later she was back; having put a movie on for the little ones, she was able to escape to a quiet place. Michelle explained how the situation in her home was chaotic. She had six children under her roof to provide for and she felt she was at a breaking point. The boys had some serious behaviors that needed addressed and they weren't being addressed because the babies had to come first. She expressed how a poopy diaper had always won over a much-needed intervention with the oldest boys. It made Michelle feel like she was doing a disservice to them.

Her proposition was to convince the State to send Rae and her two-year old brother Camden elsewhere (preferably my household). She desired to continue working with the oldest boys, Robert and Jordan. Both boys needed a great amount of attention to overcome their struggles. Camden needed to be separated because he was mimicking his brother's undesirable behaviors. If these children were to heal, their best chance was to be separated.

Astounded, I began walking through the process with Michelle about who we would need to contact to make this happen. Michelle commented that as much as she wanted to be the mother that Camden and Rae deserved, it never felt right; she never felt like she was meant be their mom. In that moment I knew the revelations I had received about Camden and Rae had been right, but needed to occur in the Lord's time. Now was my chance to take Camden, and have my baby Rae back. I shared with her my thoughts: I always had felt like I was meant to be their mother.

She said there was a hearing on Thursday she wanted Alan and I to attend. She would make arrangements with Sara to make sure we could be there. She recognized how unfair it was for the State to have taken Rae from us, and she was going to do everything she could to try and reverse that decision.

Michelle mentioned that her agency was reaching out to other homes. A few homes had already accepted the children's placement. She had the same fears I did. Would they relocate *all* the children? Would that home love and care for them like we had? I knew we had to act quickly and carefully to convince the State to do what was right for them: send Camden and Rae to us.

After our phone call, I contacted Alan with the news. Overjoyed at the chance to have Rae again, he readily agreed that we must take Camden—we had already made that decision to take him twice before. We

marked our calendar for the meeting and spent
the next several days praying and fasting. I also went to
the temple.

I met my mother on a Wednesday to do a temple
endowment session together. I prayed the entire time
that the Lord would enlighten my mind with the words
to speak in the meeting. I also prayed that he would
enlighten the minds of those overseeing the meeting. I
needed God to prompt them to listen to Michelle and I,
hear our concerns, and act in the way that would be best
for the children—separating them between our homes.

My mother noticed my heavy heart. We exited the
temple doors and she asked if I wanted to talk about
what was bothering me. I couldn't talk about it with *her*.
I didn't want to break her heart again. She had loved Rae
and had broken down much the same as I did when Rae
left. I couldn't ask her to walk this path with me.

I looked at her and selfishly whispered, "I need
Heavenly Father to answer my prayer in the way *I* want
it to be answered. Something is happening. Will you pray
and fast for my family? We need another miracle." She
couldn't end our conversation there.

"Does this have something to do with Rae?"

"I can't say right now, but *please* pray for us." I
replied. She glanced at me worriedly. I gave her a hug
and assured her that I was fine, but needed enough faith
to move a mountain. She said she would pray. We
departed the temple and I drove to pick Aubrey and
Aunna up from school.

Thursday morning dawned; Alan and I were up early going over things we might bring up during the meeting. We both tried to act as normal as we could without the girls becoming aware of our anxiety. Our appointment was at 9 a.m. so we quickly had to drop the girls off in the car rider line and book it to the L&N Building in downtown Louisville. Alan and I talked as we drove.

Our biggest concern was that the State wouldn't separate the siblings. They had denied us a sibling separation before. Would this be any different? We discussed various responses and counterarguments we might have to make depending on what the Cabinet said. We brought up the idea that if Michelle and Octavio didn't adopt Robert and Jordan, we would adopt them. My heart raced. That would mean seven kids! I had always wanted a big family, but I wasn't sure I was the kind of person that could handle it. We had to make that proposal though; it was the only way to counteroffer the Cabinet's argument to keep them all together.

The second-floor conference room was filling up. There were many people whom we had worked with in the past seated around a long oval table. Octavio sat at the end of the table and Alan and I sat next to him towards the middle. Our caseworker, Holly, slipped in beside us to represent our family. Across the table sat Sara, her supervisor Susan, and an agency caseworker Shara. In the front of the room there was a whiteboard and large easel pad for notetaking. Jessica, a Cabinet worker, sat at the head of the table to mediate the discussion.

Welcoming everyone into the room, she began the proceedings. Jessica dialed the phone numbers for Michelle and Tiffany, who was the children's therapist, to phone-conference them into the meeting since they could not attend in person. My heart pounded as Jessica began mapping out each of the children's histories on the easel next to her. She needed clarity about this sibling group. I could tell she wanted to understand what kinds of issues these children had faced and why there were so many of us sitting in this meeting who cared about these kids. She needed to organize the information we all knew. Like putting a puzzle together, each of us contributed to the list of placement histories, traumas, and mental health conditions we had witnessed from the children while in our care. I was saddened by the growing list and worried about the children's well-being. Yet, the things written did not intimidate me. I felt confident about mine and Michelle's plan. I prayed Jessica would hear our pleas.

After outlining each child's history, she turned to us and asked, "What are the options we have for these kids going forward?" Susan spoke first. I squirmed in my seat. She was the reason after all that I didn't have my Rae.

She spoke passionately about how these siblings needed to be together because they were helping one another heal from their past experiences. She said that if

Michelle and Octavio didn't feel they were capable of caring for these children any longer, she had reached out to several homes already who were capable.

One home in particular was mentioned that had a biological paraplegic daughter. It didn't sit well with me. A home containing a child with those particular medical needs, could not care for these four siblings—five including the baby. It would not be in their best interest. If Michelle thought a poopy diaper was keeping Robert and Jordan from getting needed attention, this would be setting them up for even less.

Michelle spoke up, and I was thankful. She suggested that it was not that her and Octavio were incapable of meeting their needs. They strongly felt that Robert and Jordan's needs could be met better and more effectively if they were given sole attention for a time. They needed support that smaller children in the home were preventing them from being able to receive.

Their therapist Tiffany was then questioned about their behaviors. She agreed with Michelle that Robert and Jordan could improve if they were given the attention and resources to do so. It was an odd suggestion from a therapist, and Tiffany noted it. However, if we truly were thinking about the success of the children as individuals, this separation needed to happen.

Jessica asked Michelle and Octavio what they thought should happen. Octavio took the lead this time. "We believe that Emma [Rae] should be returned to a familiar home, like the Alami's home. We also suggest that Camden go with her due to the close relationship they have developed. We would like to continue working with Robert and Jordan. We also live very close to the Alami's, so having the children see each other often will not be an issue."

Jessica turned to Sara. "Are the parents keeping their court orders?"

"No, the parents aren't even being granted visitation at the moment," she replied.

"Are we petitioning the courts for adoption?"

"Yes, and we need to find permanency for them soon. The children already know the Alami family and I feel it will be less traumatic for all the children if Camden and Emma [Rae] are placed with them."

"Are the Alami's a concurrent home?" Jessica questioned.

"Yes," Sara confirmed.

Jessica tapped the back of the marker she had been using on her cheek. "Why was this baby moved in the first place?" she asked, pointing to Rae's name on the easel. I sat up a little straighter and turned around to see Alan's face. He shook his head and reminded me to be humble and not gloat about Jessica's same realization: the injustice that had been done to Rae and us. "It would have been better for her to have remained with the Alami's and we could have prevented another disruption for the children," she concluded.

Taking a formal document with official Cabinet letterhead from a pile, she wrote as she spoke. "We are moving Camden and Emma [Rae] to the Alami's house," she stated officially. "When?" she asked.

Alan and I looked at Octavio. "I think we can work that out between us." he said.

"I'm sure we can probably do it on Saturday," Alan suggested.

"I will leave the logistics of this transition up to you," Jessica answered. "Please sign saying you agree with the plan that is being proposed." She passed around the document she had just been noting on.

Susan took the pen from Jessica and seemed reluctant, but signed the document. So did every seat around the table. I felt an abundance of joy. I had fasted, prayed, and attended the temple to plead with my Heavenly Father for Rae. My family, without knowing the specifics, had prayed earnestly for the miracle I sought because I had asked them. A mountain that had once blocked my path was moved—all because of *faith*. The Lord had heard our prayers and through faith we saw a miracle. Alan and I said a prayer of gratitude in the car afterwards. Through the grace of God, it was certain. Rae was coming home!

CHAPTER 13

Homecoming

Faith is often used as the answer to so many things.
As we face the troubles of this world, faith is what
preacher and scripture will express as the solution to all
adversities we face. We, our Heavenly Father's children,
are promised: if we "hearken unto [his] words, [he has]
prepared a blessing and an endowment for [us], if [we]
continue faithful." For He has said, "I have heard their
prayers, and will accept their offering; and it is
expedient in me that they should be brought thus far for
a trial of their faith."[20] Our faith had been tried. In every
step, Alan and I had turned to Him for guidance. We had
reluctantly tried foster care, were blessed with Aubrey,
Aunna, and then Rae. We knew the Lord had guided us
to become foster parents. Regardless of the emotional

---

[20] D&C 105:18-19

strain it put on us, we knew we were following the plan the Lord had for our family. We had Aubrey and were soon going to adopt Aunna. Since we still felt our family was incomplete, we had the faith to add more foster children in hopes of adoption: Rae.

Despite Rae's circumstance, we continued to have faith and left two placements open. We could have stopped—most people would have. We could have gladly adopted two and been done, but that was not what we knew we should do. We trusted in the Lord that he would guide us to those children who were meant to be ours—even if it was for a short time. God had undoubtably worked a miracle in our lives we did not expect to see. However, the miracle didn't happen until both Alan and I had shown the Lord—no matter what difficulties we faced—we would willingly follow Him. Like Abraham's willingness to sacrifice Isaac, it was only after we acted in faith that we saw the miracle.

We were going to have our baby back! This event could only be described as divine intervention. Things *were* going to "be better than they were before," and we were finally getting Camden! The Lord was keeping His promises.

Michelle and Octavio invited us over on Friday evening to prepare the children for the transition. They had told the boys of the decision earlier, so they could work through any negative feelings previous to our arrival. We were greeted warmly in their home and I was awestruck at how Rae had grown during the five months away from us. Her hair covered her face and she flipped it back over her head with finesse. Now, at almost eighteen months old, she had met milestones that I had missed. She was walking and talking in short sentences.

I set aside those feelings of self-pity and focused on easing myself back into her life. She was nervous around Alan and I. Clearly, she didn't remember us, which was a benefit to her because it had helped her attach to her siblings quickly. We sat down on the couch and Alan pulled out his phone. He found the pictures we had taken five months ago after her birthday party. She curiously inched towards the phone for a closer look. I could see her mind working through her eyes. She wondered why she was in those photographs.

Rae's eyes darted from the phone to Alan's face, and then to mine. Finally, she crawled up on Alan's lap. He was gaining her trust; after all, she was in his photos. When I asked to hold her, she declined. I didn't push it, and I wondered if she did, in fact, remember that day in Rachel's car. Did she hold a grudge against me? I knew I needed to be patient and let her come to me in her own time, but it was hard to restrain myself. I had missed her so much.

Camden seemed to sense something was amiss and peeked at us from around the corner of the kitchen. He stood there with his fingers in his mouth inquisitively watching us on the couch with his baby sister Rae. Things were changing, but he was too young to understand exactly what. He had seen me before, so I assumed he remembered who I was. "Hi Camden," I waved at him. He walked in, noticing I had caught him lurking. He grabbed his Dr. Seuss books off the shelf and showed me a few of his favorites.

After a few minutes, we moved to the kitchen table where the kids gathered for a sweet treat before bedtime. I sat down beside Camden. Michelle had started feeding him his cake. She had chosen to spoon feed him like an infant; it was a therapeutic intervention to help build some trust with her. She turned to me and handed me the spoon. Camden needed to become used to me—to trust me—whether he wanted to or not. I took the spoon and smiled at him as I gently picked up a bite. He smiled back shyly but took the cake I offered. He finished without an issue, and Michelle came over to wipe him up and get him ready for bed.

We discussed with Octavio the plan we had for pick up the next day. It would need to be early in the morning due to the girls' soccer games. As we were conversing, Camden came back to watch us. He was dressed and ready for bed and held out a favorite toy for me to see. I smiled and placed my hand on his. "Neat toy Camden," I responded. I knelt down in front of him to get a closer look.

Alan and I knew it was getting late and with so many preparations still to do before tomorrow, we said a simple goodbye to Rae and Camden. Michelle grabbed Camden's hand that had just been in mine and told him it was time for bed. He immediately started to tantrum. He stretched up on his toes and threw his head back. His outward behavior expressed his intuition about why Alan and I had come back into his life. Octavio picked him up to calm him.

Michelle shared with me some interventions they had done to calm him when he was throwing a tantrum. She also showed me a picture of one of the worst tantrums he had ever had. Camden had refused to eat his dinner and was red-faced, angry, and screaming; his legs had become stuck attempting to get out of his booster seat. His face scared me. Camden was known to throw excessive tantrums and I wasn't sure how I would handle that unwanted behavior. However, I knew that the Lord had commanded me to take him, so I trusted that I would be able to "accomplish the thing which he [had commanded]."[21]

Saturday morning on October 7, 2017, we headed back to Michelle and Octavio's house at nine o'clock. The girls had soccer games at two different locations, so we drove both of our vehicles. We planned on sending Camden with Alan to Aubrey's soccer game, and Rae

---

[21] 1 Nephi 3:7

would stay with me at Aunna's soccer game. I hated being separated the first hour we were placed together as a family, but it seemed to be unavoidable.

Alan and Octavio spent the first 20 minutes packing up the minivan with all of their belongings. Rae still had many possessions, but not nearly as much as what I had sent with her. I couldn't help but wonder what kinds of things Michelle had decided not to keep.

Michelle led me downstairs to the storage room. There were boxes of toys and a booster seat she offered to us for Camden. We readily accepted whatever she selflessly parted with that would make our lives easier.

It was a bitter-sweet moment as we stood in the living room together. Camden and Rae were dressed and ready to go. We stood in a circle and held hands—both our families united. Octavio said the prayer. He prayed that the Lord would watch over our family and bless us. He prayed that this move would surely, in fact, help each of these children succeed to become their best selves. We hugged and let Camden and Rae say their goodbyes.

Michelle leaned down to Rae and whispered, "Love you."

"Love you" Rae repeated. Alan picked her up and she waved at them through the glass storm door, while I grabbed Camden's hand and led him outside. The boys followed us out onto the front porch to watch us leave. Robert stood there with watered eyes, while Jordan hid his teary face behind Michelle.

These boys were hurt. Camden had always been with them. What would they do now when he wasn't around?

We promised we would see them soon for a visit. Robert and Jordan seemed to take comfort in that fact. It helped them cope with the difficult circumstance we were placing them in. I heard Michelle ask Jordan how he was feeling. I knew as we walked away that she had prepared him for this separation. I'm sure she reminded him that he knew us, so he should know that we would take care of Camden and Rae. He didn't have to worry about that. They hugged one another and went back inside as we pulled out of the driveway.

❋❋❋

"Hello Family!" we exclaimed as we video messaged our family right after the soccer games. "This is Camden, and this is Emma Rae. Surprise!"

My dad responded with his own video message. He was in tears. Rae was back home and our joy was full. We were a family again; and I thanked the Lord for this miracle.

CHAPTER 14

Camden and Faith

Rae adjusted beautifully. From the minute she stepped into our home, it seemed familiar to her. She especially liked how her picture was hanging in the hallway. I had put it there a month earlier when I had healed enough emotionally to look at her in photos and videos again. I thought that it would hang there forever and would somehow freeze her in time at twelve months old. It was a silly thought, but I wanted to remember Rae exactly the way she was when she left. Now I held this beautiful eighteen-month-old version of Rae in my arms! She wasn't an infant, but she was still Rae.

During this period of adjustment, Aunna officially joined our family. On October 10, 2017, three days after Camden and Rae returned, we went to the court house for her big day. We attended the temple a few days later

and added her to
our eternal family.
She let go of the
anxiety she had
harbored for so
long about her
future. She knew
she would be taken
care of, safe, and

free from those who had caused her harm and heartache.

Alan and I celebrated our growing family. I said a
prayer of gratitude that night to the Lord for being
mindful of us. We had two beautiful daughters that
were officially ours, and more yet to come. I marveled at
how the Lord had watched over my children before they
came to us. He had led us to them. He had intervened to
bring Rae back, with Camden. I thanked Him fervently
for bringing my family together.

***

Camden played easily with Aubrey, Aunna, and
Rae. We spent two weeks after the transition with no
major issues. I started to wonder what had changed this
boy, until one day I realized our honeymoon period was
over. He was going to be a little trickier to parent than
the girls.

I had sat Camden and Rae down for lunch with a
bowl of macaroni-and-cheese. Rae sat peacefully in her
high chair gulping the noodles whole. Camden crossed
his arms. I coaxed him to take a bite of his lunch. Then,

with all the fury of a two (almost three) year-old, he screamed, punched, and kicked his legs about. I was baffled. Here was the behavior we had been warned about unfolding before me in all its rage.

I started to count and breathe with him; he refused to count with me and became even louder. Huge tears started streaming down his face and he pounded his booster chair with such force that I had to catch the bowl of noodles before they spilled on the floor. I set the bowl back on the table and tried another calming strategy. Meanwhile, Rae sat nonchalant in her chair still gulping noodles.

Nothing seemed to be working to calm Camden down. I got out my camera and started filming him; my only option was to simply let him cry it out. I filmed him for 20 seconds. I would show him the video later and try to use it as a teaching moment; plus, I wanted Alan to see what everyone had warned us about. I understood he was experiencing some big emotions. I knew this behavior wasn't due to a bowl of macaroni-and-cheese.

I cleaned Rae up a few minutes later as the last of Camden's pouts quieted. I walked over to him and gave him the biggest hug. I told him I cared about him and I was going to keep him safe. I wanted to tell him he didn't have to go anywhere else—that he would stay with me forever—but the Spirit restrained me. I didn't have the power to make that decision. I had learned that lesson months earlier.

He let me wipe his tears. Unable to communicate what was really bothering him, he grabbed his spoon and tried to eat his macaroni-and-cheese. I took the spoon from him and fed him like a baby. Each move from house to house had taken a toll on this sweet boy. He had missed his babyhood. He had been asked to act like his older brothers long before he was capable. I felt sorry for him.

As a consequence for his tantrum, he wasn't able to get a pom-pom for his reward chart. I told him that if he wanted his prize on the fireplace mantle, a Hot Wheels car, he would have to behave better and earn enough pom-poms for it. He nodded—a little disappointed. I showed him a few seconds of the video I took. I told him that children aren't allowed to act that way in my house, but I still loved him. I held high expectations and he could choose to be better.

Later that night we snuggled in bed. I read him his favorite book, Green Eggs and Ham. We lay there a minute together and I gazed upon his little face. If I could only express the love I had for him, I was sure he would trust me more. I wished I could. I wanted to take away all his hurt. I leaned down and planted a kiss on his forehead. "I love you Camden, will you be my baby boy?" I asked.

His eyes brightened and he smiled. "Oh yes!" he exclaimed. I gave him a squeeze, turned on the nightlight, and closed the bedroom door. Why had I asked him that? I wasn't sure, but I didn't feel wrong about doing it. It had made him feel loved and that's what he needed right now.

The next several days were better. No tantrums at all. Rae and Camden were normal children, they played together, and fought together like a normal pair of siblings do. Camden earned his toy car and another small toy replaced it on the mantle for him to earn. He only tried to tantrum on two other occasions that month, but a gentle reminder of losing his pom-pom quickly hushed his pouting.

We visited Robert and Jordan weekly. Each visit was filled with excitement to see one another. They built block towers with Camden and played house with Rae. Sometimes they invited Aubrey and Aunna to join in the fun. I tried to keep the girls separate—occupying them with other fun things, so it wouldn't feel like they were being left out.

I could get a sense of the boys' progress at these visits and gained insights about their personalities. Robert was athletic and competitive. He touted fairness often and would let me know when he thought things were unjust. Jordan was loud, rambunctious, and a provoker. He was also sensitive, service-oriented, and thoughtful of others. He was the one I had trouble figuring out.

***

Faith was born on November 6, 2017. Sissy went to the hospital to witness the birth. She called me at 1:30 a.m. with the news and texted me many pictures. I was excited to have my little girl who had spoken to me from Heaven finally out of the womb. Sissy said that she was healthy, but was currently being hooked up to morphine. She was starting the process of weaning off opiates. I longed to see and hold Faith, but I had to be patient. I wouldn't be allowed to come to the hospital until my name was on an official visitation list.

It took the State a week to put mine and Alan's name on that list, but on November 12, 2017 I finally managed to go to the hospital at 9 p.m. to see her. Alan had already seen her earlier after work, the hospital just being a block away from his office building. He went from five to six and I scheduled my time to see her after dinner and bedtime routines. We had to manage our time around the other four children at home. I was jealous that he was able to hold Faith before I was, but I understood our circumstance.

Faith's birth father was in her room when I arrived. Not wanting to cause a scene, I asked if I could wait in another location while they asked him to leave. Nine to ten o'clock was my scheduled daily time to see Faith; he was able to be there all other hours besides Alan's.

I waited in a nurse's station off the side entrance to the NICU. After several minutes a nurse came to retrieve me. She said that Faith's birth dad was displeased and grunted derogatory remarks all the way out of the NICU. He had even whispered to baby Faith before laying her back in her crib, "Your other mother is here to see you. Cry your a** off for her." He had laughed smugly, but compliantly left the room.

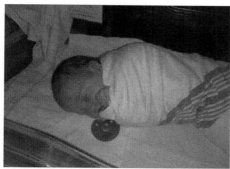 I tried to keep my cool. This situation was delicate. I needed to keep myself composed to prove how prepared I was to care for this child. Social workers and nurses took notes about what happened in Faith's room. I knew they were watching me and I wasn't about to give them an excuse to recommend Faith to another foster home.

Faith was a sweet baby. She looked so precious and innocent swaddled up. Her room was dimly lit and there was soft music playing from a sound machine on a side table.

Shortly after I made it to her bedside, her night nurse came up to me with a bottle and two syringes. She said she would give Faith her medicines, but asked if I would like to feed her. I happily took the bottle and watched the nurse place the medicine on the inside of her cheek. She mentioned Faith had scored a five that day on her withdrawal assessment, her best number to date. It broke my heart to see her symptoms. She had tremors, tight muscles, sweating, and poor suction on her bottle. She was given morphine to cope with some of these symptoms at just a week old!

I carefully took Faith from the nurse and placed the bottle into her mouth. She quietly tried to suck without opening her eyes. I caught the excess milk dribbling out under her chin with a cloth while the nurse made a note to try a different nipple for the next feeding. Minutes passed as I fawned on her; the bottle slowly drained. I sat her up and held her jaw between my fingers to burp her. She was so little and fragile. I patted her back until she had passed all her exuberant air.

Gently, I laid her down on my legs. She was quite awake now. Her little eyes rolled around looking at the light filtering in from the doorway. I prayed over her that she would be able to wean from the drugs easily, so she could come home quickly. I felt the Spirit testify that He was in control of this child and she would be all right. I sang, "I Am a Child of God" to her. I told her that I had waited for her, and when she was adopted, we had already picked out a name for her: Allie Faith. She grinned when I mentioned her name. I knew that was what she was meant to be called; it had taken a great deal of *faith* for us to get here. I rocked her to sleep; I sang as I rocked. Her mommy was here. All was well.

CHAPTER 15

Steadfast Faith

Extra precautions are taken in the NICU, especially as the weather changes. I went daily to see Faith, but as cold weather set in, I was required to wash my hands thoroughly and then given hand sanitizer before I was allowed entrance. The weather change had made the perfect environment for sickness to spread, so this extensive hand washing became a needful routine.

Faith had been in the hospital three weeks. Soft music was playing, the lights were dimmed, and she was fast asleep in her crib. I peered at her not wanting to wake her just yet. Her nurse on duty came in with two syringes and a bottle, just like she did every night.

She inserted the first syringe into Faith's cheek and asked me about my experience in foster care. I shared with her a little about the children I had in my home and the plans the State and I had for Faith going forward. The nurse asked, "Do you have medically fragile training?"

My brow furrowed. Why was she asking me this? Had some change occurred that would cause my Allie Faith to be classified as medically fragile? "I don't," I replied honestly.

"But you have her siblings?"

"Yes, we do."

"I feel like I need to warn you." She explained how a couple she had met recently were asked to take a baby home from this particular NICU unit. Yet, these foster parents were unable to do so. They had not obtained medically fragile training to administer the child's medication. She indicated that Faith was on the same medication. My heart sank.

I had fought the State for Rae and her siblings. *I* wanted this baby, Sissy wanted *us* to have this baby, and—most importantly—the *Lord* wanted us to have her. I wondered if the State would push the issue. I remembered how they had made a rash decision for Rae based on nothing but a man-made law and a case file. Not this time; not again. Sissy, Alan, and I were real people who loved and cared a great deal about these kids. We had been in a tricky position before with Rae and had not been listened to. Would the State make an exception for us now?

I fed Faith as I thought about what the nurse had said. Doubt began flooding my mind. Would the State frustrate Faith's plan to be with us? I had heard a voice dictate from heaven that she was *mine*.

I prayed over Faith and placed her back into her crib to sleep. I hastily exited the hospital. I was upset. Worried tears began streaming down my face before I hit the lobby. I practically ran to my car. I called my mother.

My mom had always been there for me—time and again. She had already talked me through countless highs and lows as I navigated the foster system. I was grateful for her willingness to listen when I needed her. She picked up the phone and hearing my breathing on the other end knew instantly that something was wrong. I told her about the conversation I had with the nurse. I needed Faith. I couldn't let her go.

My mother's response was rational. She suggested that perhaps the nurse had to warn me so that I could fight this battle before it became an issue with the State. I told her my worries concerning the State and their decision making. She agreed that, given their history, they might place Faith elsewhere—which didn't ease my fears.

I became distraught. I couldn't let *my* baby slip away from me. Not again. I recklessly pulled out of the parking lot and began the drive home. My mother let me go; she begged me to focus on my driving and to be safe. I hung up unsatisfied and without comfort.

Honestly, I'm not sure how I made it home that night. I wasn't paying attention to anything or anyone else on the road. I was completely caught up in the worry that I was going to lose Faith. I couldn't trust the State, and I had made an enemy along my way in my fight for Rae. Susan, Sara's supervisor, had denied our petitions to keep Rae. She had only consented to allow her to come back into our home through pressure from social workers during her hearing. I was apprehensive about what she would do when she found out Faith was on a controlled substance. In my mind, I already knew the answer, and I didn't like it.

Fear does not come from the Lord. It is a tool Satan uses for deception, distraction, and discouragement.[22] I was feeling all those things. I felt the State was being deceptive about their plans for Faith, and I was discouraged, due to my past experience, that I was powerless to change it. That night I felt the power of the adversary in full force. He was trying to distract me. He was trying to make me feel useless and undeserving. I knew his ploy. I tried to heed my mother's council and choose to see this as a warning rather than let Satan attack my faith.

Alan said we should make Sara aware of the situation. She had experience with us, knew we wanted these children, and that we loved them unconditionally. I called her early the next morning. She said she would speak with her supervisor, Susan, and make the recommendation for Faith to continue as planned (to our

---

22 Johnson, Peter M. *Power to Overcome the Adversary*. Ensign. November 2019. p110.

home) when discharged. I still pleaded with Heavenly Father that Faith would be placed with us. I prayed with all the faith and vigor I could conjure that Sara wouldn't fail us.

Later that afternoon, I received a phone call from the hospital. The hospital social worker had heard of our case, so I assumed Sara had informed her about my concerns. She had looked at the logs and saw Alan and I had shown up almost every night to care for Faith; we even had come on Thanksgiving Day to see this precious baby girl. She was impressed by our dedication to this child. She also understood that we had Faith's siblings in our care; therefore, she was making a recommendation on our behalf to the state of Kentucky for us to take Faith when she was discharged—even if she was considered to be medically fragile.

I took courage and counted it as another blessing from the Lord. What would have happened if I had not been proactive and heeded the warning from the nurse? Perhaps something, perhaps nothing. Yet I held on to my faith in the Savior and the plan that Heavenly Father had for baby Faith. He was working miracles. People I hadn't even met before were working behind the scenes to ensure these children stayed together in *our* home. I sent a prayer of gratitude immediately to heaven. Her recommendation was invaluable.

Faith came home on November 29, 2017. Faith had managed to overcome her tremors and sucking issues. However, she still struggled with sweating and some muscle tightness. The hospital sent home two weeks' worth of medication, but the dosage was small. After that time, Faith would be healthy enough to not rely on it. She would no longer be classified by the State as medically fragile. She was stable enough to be home with us and I was thrilled.

My mother came to help Alan and I as we brought her home from the hospital. She had gotten the girls to school that morning while Alan and I took care of things at the hospital. Our church family brought us meals which gave us time to focus on our kids and new baby. We felt God's favor and I was already seeing how things were "better than they were before."

***

In a matter of two months, we had quickly outgrown our three-bedroom, one-bath house. We sensed we would all be a little more comfortable with at least one more bathroom and another bedroom. Looking at our finances, we concluded that it was time. We could upgrade to a slightly bigger home. I began looking for things online, but nothing ever came up for sale that satisfied my taste or fit our family just right. Most of the houses on the market needed work, and a lot of it. We didn't think we had the time to take on a housing project with so many kids, so we decided to go with a new-build.

We signed a contract on a 2100-ish square foot house with four bedrooms, three bathrooms, and a large unfinished basement in which we had plans to finish later on. We were excited to embark on this chapter of our lives and recognized again the Lord's hand in allowing us to purchase a house that was nicer, and sixty years newer than what we were in before.

We had five beautiful children whom we loved dearly. Their case was being petitioned for adoption in court. We were building a new house in a pleasant part of Louisville. I never imagined in such a short amount of time that we would be the recipients of such blessings. The Lord has said, "prove me now herewith...if I will not open you the windows of heaven, and pour you out a blessing, that there shall not be room enough to receive it."[23] We were being blessed for our faith, and this was merely a taste of what the Lord was preparing for us.

---

[23] Malachi 3:10

CHAPTER 16

Visitation

Our story is one of faith, patience, and sacrifice. Turning our hearts completely to the Lord required a culmination of small and large acts that mandated our hearts to change and to choose Him. Through these sacred experiences, Alan and I encountered firsthand that "the Lord requireth the heart and a willing mind."[24] Faith necessitates laying aside our desires and turning our control over to Him absolutely.

Regardless of having a home full of children, which we would have never foreseen possible at the start of our marriage, there were still trials that dotted our path along the way. We had already endured several hardships in between the happy moments of uniting our family. However, I always confided in the Lord. I took

---

24 Doctrine and Covenants 64:34

my fears to Him and let the peace of His Spirit calm me often.

One of my hardest experiences as a mother was being unable to fix my children's hurts. Three months after Faith was brought home from the hospital (January 2018), the judge ordered parent visitation again. The children had gone months without seeing their birth parents and had made excellent progress. Faith was off her medication and was developing properly. Her siblings had improved behaviors and were attaching to their respective caregivers better than the caseworkers had anticipated. Seeing their birth parents came with a risk of behavioral relapse.

Visitation brought a whole new set of problems and trials. I took the three children to Sara's office. Their birth parents entered the foyer and I tried to smile as I stood there with *my* babies. Their birth mom smiled back. She looked clean and about the same as she had at our last encounter. Their birth dad ignored me and looked thuggish. His pants hung low and exposed his boxers around his waist. He wore a wife beater and had a gold chain around his neck. I held tightly to Rae on my hip and held Camden's little hand. Faith sat asleep in her car seat on the floor.

Camden didn't recognize his birth mother at first. She went up to him and spoke a few minutes with him. He must have decided to trust her because he let her pick him up. I held tighter to Rae. I answered any questions their birth mother asked and tried to be kind; I remembered I had been commanded to be meek. I reminded myself again: "She [was] a child of God, and He loved her too." Keeping this eternal perspective kept me humble during these hours of turmoil. Sara came out to invite the birth parents and children into the playroom. Rae held tightly to me. Every inch of me wanted to grab the children and run. I couldn't subject them to these people—the same people who had hurt them so terribly.

Camden had been placed in kinship care due to a burn on his thigh at around fifteen months old. Robert and Jordan had been taken also after multiple allegations of untreated illnesses and poor hygiene. There was also verbal and physical abuse that was factored into the decision to remove them from their parent's custody. Rae and Faith had been removed on account of being born addicted to substances. They both had to be put on morphine to overcome the pain of weaning. It was difficult to keep my head clear in these moments and act in accordance with the law. I had to send them to their visit. I was obligated to comply.

Camden hesitated for one second, but Robert and Jordan persuaded him to go. They both said, "Camden, this is mom and dad." They said it like it was natural and good that they should be with them. My heart ached at those words. I could tell Camden was confused, but he walked willingly with his brothers. Faith was quickly grabbed by her birth dad, who woke her up, unbuckled her without asking, and ripped her from the carrier. She was too young to understand.

Rae stayed glued to me. She was silently begging me not to make her go with these people. Her birth mom came over and offered her hands out. I reluctantly placed Rae in her arms. I turned around quickly to walk away—listening to Rae's screams fading behind me.

I ran to my vehicle and broke. This wasn't fair to Rae, or to any of these children. The parents had not actually been compliant in their court orders. They were still using substances; not one drug test had been clean—not ever. Why were we subjecting these children to these parents who clearly could not put their priorities in order? It was the judge.

Sara had warned me about the decisions this judge had made in other cases. She was very pro-parent—no matter how much evidence was collected against them. This judge was naïve to think that people would actually change just because she ordered them to. She gave birth parents more chances than she should have, and seemed deaf to the Cabinet's petitions to stop visitation. The negative impact on the children was severe. In the judge's mind, it made sense that birth parents should see their kids. If they weren't in jail, then she thought they had a right to visit with them.

I knew better. The Lord has revealed that parents "have a solemn responsibility to love and care for each other and for their children...[and] have a sacred duty to rear their children in love and righteousness, to provide for their physical and spiritual needs, and to teach them to love and serve one another, observe the commandments of God, and be law-abiding citizens wherever they live."[25] Their birth parents had never cared for one another or their children. Domestic violence and neglect had abounded under their guardianship. There was never an instance where they had taught their children the commandments of God or to obey the law.

Again, my mother never failed answering the phone when I sought her compassion. I had dialed her number and related the event that left me tormented. I had walked away from Rae *again*. She didn't deserve this. I longed for the day when I could explain to her that I didn't have a choice. I wanted to run away with her. I wanted to save her from those who would harm her.

My dear mother listened intently. She gave me strength; many times, realizing it or not, the Spirit spoke through her to relay the things I needed to hear. This was a step I had to take. I had to prove to the judge that these parents were incompetent. Letting them have an hour of supervised time was what was needed to prove it. Sara could gather evidence as she watched them to further attest the Cabinet's recommendation for adoption.

I entered the building an hour later for pick up. Rae ran and hugged me tight around the legs. She showed me a small toy her birth dad had given her.

---

25 *The Family: A Proclamation to the World.* 1995. Retrieved from web 4 December 2019. https://www.churchofjesuschrist.org/topics/family-proclamation?lang=eng&old=true

Sara pulled me aside to tell me that Rae had cried most of the visit, but had calmed down about twenty minutes before I showed up. Faith was disheveled from being played with and passed around frequently. Her hairbow was missing, which upset me. It proved they had been careless with her. Yet, I kept my thoughts to myself.

I buckled Faith into her carrier, put on Camden and Rae's jackets, and stepped outside. Sara called me several minutes later as we drove home. Their birth parents had not been appropriate. There were many things said that should not have been—i.e., obscenities, rudeness, and inapt promises were made—promises they could not keep. Sara wanted me to know this in case one of the children said something that evening. We would have to work through any misconceptions they might have formed, like going back to live with their parents.

I bathed the kids when we got home. I meticulously scrubbed their little cheeks, mentally and physically wiping away the loveless kisses their birth parents had left there. After dressing them all again, I ushered everyone around the table for dinner. Camden was being a little more difficult than usual. He didn't want a bath, he didn't want his dinner, and he didn't want to go to bed. I figured this was just usual three-year-old behavior. However, time taught me differently. A pattern began to form.

Once per week we went to birth parent visits. Each time Rae refused to go and had to be taken from my arms or pried off my legs. Camden always threw a tantrum after every visit. I began to see this wasn't just "terrible threes." Camden was crying out for help.

On our way to visitation one week, he said, "Mom, George has one dad, but I have two." I was astonished by his observation. It was clear to me he had been watching other families around us. He had noticed that most children, even his best friend George, had *one* father. We had never spoken about Camden's birth dad before. "I mean, I have a dad, but I have my other dad too," he affirmed. He spoke well and I was stunned at his comprehension. He understood most kids have one dad and one mom. He was telling me plainly that he had two dads and I sensed he wanted to know why.

I honestly didn't know how to respond to him, so I waited a minute and glanced at his face in my rearview mirror a few times before I spoke. "Camden," I began, "I love you. You live with me because I am able to take care of you. I am able to keep you safe." I paused a minute to let him process what I was saying and to prepare him for my next statement. I believe in being honest with my kids, so I felt like I should be honest now. "Your 'other dad' is not able to keep you safe or take care of you right now," I concluded.

"Yes, he can! My other dad is strong and can kill somebody if they hurt me. He can even kill the police."

"Camden, the police are good guys," I gently corrected him.

"No, they tried to get my other dad."

"What do you mean?" I asked intently. Something

was obviously bothering this kid. I caught a glimpse of him again in the mirror trying to figure out how he was processing certain events.

"He had to run away from the police so they won't take him to jail," he stated. I recalled how the police had shown up to escort a man from the building last week. His birth dad had run and hid out at the McDonalds across the street for a time before showing up halfway through the visit. Later, we discovered there was a warrant out for his arrest, so his birth dad assumed the police were there for him. Camden either had watched this happen or his birth dad had told him this. I suspected the latter.

"Why would they take him to jail?" I probed him.

"The bad guys were trying to get him!" Camden raised his voice clearly frustrated that I wasn't getting something.

"You mean the police? The police are good guys. The police take bad guys to jail."

"No, mom." I could see his mind working as he tried to give me more information. He tried to understand what that meant about his birth dad. He couldn't make the connection, so the conversation ended. A minute later we arrived at Sara's office and again Rae cried as I pried her from myself. I had a taste of the inaptness of these visits only minutes ago. This was wrong. It was weighing heavily on Camden. He was developing misconstructions about right and wrong. He didn't know who the *good guys* were. Did he think that I was a *bad guy*? After all, I was involved in keeping him from his "other dad."

CHAPTER 17

Over and Over Again

Most parents, starting with their first child, develop parenting strategies as their child grows. They slowly add to their family and more expertise is gained as children reach certain stages of development. Alan and I were both thrown into the fire of parenting. In three years, Alan and I went from zero to five children. The phrase "instant family" became meaningful to us. There were times when I literally had no idea how to handle a situation. I would honestly look at my children and say, "Daddy and I are going to discuss this choice you made and we will let you know the consequence." As the months went on and we got to know our kids, parenting became easier. I didn't have to counsel with Alan as often, because we became acquainted with what discipline strategies worked for our children.

Camden's tantrums were always right on schedule.

After every birth parent visit, he would become stubborn, cross, and irritable. He lacked his normal rationalizing skills and became a tumult of temper. One evening as I fought this battle, for what seemed like the hundredth time, I paused to ponder my parenting strategies. His behavior chart had become an ineffective tool after visits. I had warned Camden of losing his pom-pom or prize, but it still did not eliminate his behavior.

I decided to pick him up and said calmly, "Camden, I love you." I held him tight. His crying was hushed, stomping ceased, and his arms fell limp. He knew that I loved him. He knew that he should not tantrum, but he couldn't help it. Things were out-of-control in his life; he wanted to control something. I rocked him like a baby several seconds and let him decide when he wanted up out of my arms.

He quickly looked up at me, ready to put his feet back on the floor. Again, I said, "Camden, I love you," and added, "you still *have* to make good choices, even when you don't want to."

"Do I get my pom-pom?" he asked, referring to his behavior chart while eyeing the prize on the fireplace mantle.

"No," I said firmly, "you threw a tantrum." I gave him one last squeeze and said, "but I love you." Disappointed he looked at the floor. He didn't argue, which told me he understood the consequence did not change despite the adversity he was facing.

Tiffany, Camden's therapist, was frank with me. She told me that Camden wouldn't cease from having these meltdowns until visitation was eliminated. Yet, birth parent visitation continued no matter how hard I fought it. I had sent emails to the children's guardian ad litem, the siblings' court appointed representative for their case, phone called both Sara and Tiffany to report each meltdown, and even asked Tiffany to write a letter of recommendation to the judge that visits be stopped. The birth parents behaved inappropriately, attended visits inconsistently, and lied to their children regularly by making promises they couldn't keep. Visitation continued regardless of my or Sara's efforts.

My sweet Camden became less obedient as these visits prolonged. I researched various therapeutic methods to find a solution for his lack of listening. One such method was having Special Play Time. Once a week we held Special Play Time for thirty minutes. Sometimes we held it in Tiffany's office, other times we did it at home. I set a timer and placed toys on a rug. We played on that rug and, for those thirty minutes, Camden was in charge; he told *me* what to do. If he told me I had to stand on one leg and jump for one minute, I did it. If he asked me to eat my pretend soup with a spoon (which was actually a fork), I called that fork a spoon and did it. I gave him complete *control.* He needed a little more of that in his life.

It wasn't a miracle solution to our problem. He was still difficult to parent, but it did improve his obedience and listening a great deal. I persevered with faith that one day Camden would be better. Visitation couldn't last forever; the judge would eventually have to make a decision, and all the evidence being collected was indicating parental rights would be terminated.

Faith was growing healthily and meeting all of her developmental milestones. She was rolling, reaching for toys, and teething. She surprised the Neonatology office with each check-up. She had issues at birth with muscular strength and was sent to a pediatric physical therapist for a time, but quickly graduated the program without much effort. She was overcoming obstacles and figuring things out on her own. Her mental strength and stamina were helping her overcome problems others would have foreseen as major hinderances.

At seven months she began recognizing faces. She knew who her daddy and mommy were: Alan and I. Faith wouldn't allow anyone else to hold her, so visitation became hard on her too.

It wasn't just Rae being pried from my body each week. Both Faith and Rae cried at being taken from me. I became angry at their birth dad and struggled to hide my emotions at times. Whenever I would arrive, he would immediately grab Faith out of my arms. She would scream and cry in protest, but each time I would have to muster up the courage to walk away. It made me sick inside. I knew her little eyes were watching me leave her.

I knew she was scared.

Her birth dad wore an expression of smugness and triumph. I didn't have any rights to his kids. He was still their legal parent. He knew it, and it thrilled him to see me so upset. I wanted to punch him in the nose!

I quickly ran to my minivan to hideout until the dreaded hour had passed. I always called my mother. She continued to be a sure foundation when things became difficult. She was always there to ease my pain and cried many tears with me due to those horrible visits.

Faith, Rae, and Camden grew. As the months went by, both girls relived the trauma of visitation over, and over, and over again. Over, and over, and over again I pried the girls off of me, listened to their screams as I walked away, and dialed my mother for comfort in my minivan. Over, and over, and over again, I fought that same battle with Camden—using every coping technique I had learned from Tiffany to bring him out of his anger.

By September, the screaming and the fighting with Camden was taking its toll on me. I was done. I couldn't endure this torture any longer. I called Sara. I told her something had to change. I couldn't take them to visitation any longer. It was wrong to subject these children to this torture each week and I was tired of driving them to see people who clearly didn't care about them. The birth parents were not keeping their court orders. It was obvious they had very little remorse for what they had done.

Sara heard my qualms, yet begged me to wait one more month. The termination trial was set for the end of October. I needed to give her time to gather evidence and it wouldn't look good if we defied court orders right before trial. We had to endure a little while longer, so the judge wouldn't have a reason to delay termination. I knew she was right. I had to continue a little while longer. Knowing this didn't stop me from making it perfectly clear: If rights were not terminated in October, we would have to do something else for visitation, because I was done. I needed out. These kids needed out.

CHAPTER 18

More Revelation

Heavenly Father knows the limits of our abilities. Oftentimes we have more strength than we think we do. I was at my breaking point. I had Camden, Rae, and Faith for almost a year, without any indication from the judge that she was planning on terminating parental rights. I loved these babies and couldn't imagine my life without them. I had to rely on the Savior and the example of His obedience to get through what I felt was the homestretch to adoption. The Savior said, "In me ye might have peace. In the world ye shall have tribulation: but be of good cheer; I have overcome the world."[26] I knew that He understood my sullenness, but was also teaching me along the way. I consciously chose to wait on Him and have faith in His promises.

---

[26] John 16:33

I love my children. Each of them brings a light into my life that can't be replicated or replaced. Their spirits resonate with my spirit and I feel an indescribable connection to them. They were each meant to be in our family; it was God's plan undoubtedly. I had felt the Holy Ghost testify to me concerning each of them. I was in awe at how the Lord gathered my children and how many small things had happened that brought about great miracles. Each time the Lord revealed an action Alan and I should take, no matter how small, we followed. It became easier to hear His directions and follow His promptings as we continually tried to act on them.

Aubrey and Aunna had returned to school as summer tapered and autumn set in. I found ways to entertain the little ones during the day. I did as much as I could to tire them out for naps, so I could enjoy some time for myself. One beautiful day I took Camden, Rae, and Faith to a splash pad at the park before the city shut it down for the winter. Camden and Rae played together under a stream of water leaking from a plastic frog who spouted it like a tongue catching a fly in mid-air. I sat with Faith nearby, splashing in the shallow puddles on the concrete. Soon, a set of brothers joined us on the nearby playground. There were three boys. Two were about the same age as Robert and Jordan and the third was about a year older than Camden. Camden quickly ditched Rae and hurried over towards them.

I watched him as he excitedly joined their game.

He seemed to fit right in with their roughhousing—playing ninjas and rolling around in the mulch. I observed him from a distance enjoying his newfound friends. They seemed to be filling a void in his life that he was missing. For thirty minutes I noted his happy disposition. Pondering on this, I felt the Spirit say, "Camden needs his brothers." I knew he missed Robert and Jordan, but I didn't know how to act on this revelation. I knew I needed to give Camden more time with his brothers, but was unsure about what Michelle and Octavio would allow.

Meanwhile, the Lord was already working on Robert and Jordan. About a week later, Michelle pulled me aside after dropping off the kids at a birth parent visit. She expressed her love for Robert and Jordan, but was troubled about their future. Termination was soon and the boys would have to be adopted. This idea had weighed heavily on Michelle and Octavio. We agreed these kids needed permanency, so she asked Alan and I both to come over that night to discuss something with us—a decision she and Octavio had already made.

I called Alan at work on the car ride home. Michelle had acted odd. If her and Octavio didn't step up and care for Robert and Jordan, who would? It was true they had been difficult to manage, and their case was frustrating. I wondered aloud if Michelle and Octavio had run out of stamina. As we discussed this, a peaceful feeling arose in my heart. The answer was clear. Alan and I both received the revelation: They were not going to adopt Robert and Jordan. We were. I felt the Spirit confirm this decision was right. Alan agreed. It had been the plan all along. Robert and Jordan were meant to be our sons. They just needed a little extra help to get there.

We dropped Aubrey, Aunna, Camden, and Rae off at my friend Shayla's house to play that night. Faith stayed with us. We didn't want to traumatize her again the same day, since visitation had only been a few hours before. Michelle and Octavio welcomed us in, as always, and we went straight down into the basement. Robert and Jordan were distracted watching a movie in the living room. They sensed something was up. It was unusual for us to be over without it being someone's birthday or a sibling visit; more unusual that we were barricading ourselves in the basement so we would not be overheard.

Alan and I took a seat on the sofa and I placed Faith on the floor to crawl around. Michelle dragged some toys over to distract her. Octavio sat across from us on the floor. We looked up at them eager to hear whatever plan they had thought of. They glanced at one another, not sure who should start talking first.

Octavio began, "We have been doing a lot of praying about these kids. We feel..." he paused. It was hard for him to explain, this was a prompting from the Lord he was describing. I knew it, and I wondered if he was hesitant out of fear of what Alan and I would think. "We feel it best that we should not adopt the boys," he struggled to say. Michelle helped him continue.

"We love the boys, but adoption never sat well with us. We feel we aren't meant to do it. We wanted to tell you because this decision is going to affect your family."

Alan and I glanced at each other and smiled. We knew the answer. We had offered to adopt them many months before when we were given the opportunity to have Rae back, and it had been revealed to us before we had sat down with Michelle and Octavio—before we knew with certainty adoption was going to be the topic of our discussion. We could do this. We had been preparing for this scenario. Robert and Jordan had been preparing to join our family through the efforts of Michelle and Octavio.

We couldn't have handled the boy's behaviors when they first entered foster care. There were too many issues. The Lord knew our strengths, yet also our weaknesses. He has said, He "will not suffer you to be tempted above that ye are able; but will with the temptation also make a way to escape, that ye may be able to bear it."[27] We couldn't take Robert and Jordan the way they were before. However, through our Heavenly Father's love, He made a way for Robert and Jordan to come to our family. Michelle and Octavio were *my* unspoken prayer. Their efforts had permitted us to be able to have Robert and Jordan, so we could *bear* them. All of us understood this now.

---

[27] 1 Corinthians 10:13

On Thursday, September 23, 2018 we met together, in the same room that we had fought for Camden and Rae a year prior, for another facilitated meeting with social workers and a representative of the Cabinet. It was difficult to describe to the Cabinet the reason for wanting to put the boys back with their siblings. It was difficult to put into logical words the revelation from the Spirit that all four of us foster parents had received. We didn't have a rational explanation as to why we wanted to break up a working, loving, placement. God had asked us to.

The facilitator listened to what we said, yet immediately following our reasoning, he attacked Michelle and Octavio. He conjured up his own rationalization to make sense of what we were saying. He said to them, "You must not understand the boys' diagnoses. They cannot help themselves." He accused them of "not [being] able to manage and handle the boys' traumatic behaviors." Michelle and Octavio protested that this was not the case. They had worked hard and consistently with Robert and Jordan. Each boy had learned how to make good choices in their care. They could control their behaviors, this facilitator refused to listen to that fact.

I felt sorry for Michelle and Octavio. After several accusatory remarks, they fell silent, taking the false reprimand with grace. Opposing his words did not seem to change what this facilitator thought about them. They were being persecuted for doing what they had been prompted by the Holy Ghost to do. Jesus Christ has said, "Blessed are ye, when men shall revile you, and persecute you, and shall say all manner of evil against you falsely, for my sake. Rejoice, and be exceeding glad: for great is your reward in heaven."[28] I knew what this facilitator was criticizing them for wasn't true. They had taught them enough. They had been able to do the work that I was unable to do. They had helped my sons, and I was grateful.

After the facilitator finished his belittling remarks towards Michelle and Octavio, he signed the papers to place Robert and Jordan in our home. He agreed with Alan and my argument: The least traumatic thing for these boys is to be reunited with their siblings in a home that had committed to love, care for, and ultimately adopt them.

We picked up Robert and Jordan the very next evening. We met Friday night at Michelle and Octavio's house to gather part of their things and make the transition. It was difficult watching them say goodbye. I could feel the love they had for their foster parents. Robert

---

[28] Matthew 5:11-12

burst into tears. I hugged him and tried to comfort him. I wanted to tell him that he would never have to move again—this was his final stop—but I couldn't promise him that. Too much had happened in my experience with foster care to make promises that I didn't have the power to keep. I wanted them to know that I cared about them and would fight for them, more than anyone had ever fought for them in their lives. I wanted to be their mother.

✱✱✱

Now that we had seven children, it became necessary to find a vehicle to safely transport all of us together. We moved some money out of our savings, so we could make this important purchase. Alan had found

a fifteen-passenger van on a used car lot, so Saturday was spent purchasing our third vehicle. I had never driven such a large vehicle before, and I was nervous at the thought. I would be driving it most of the time, hauling these children to their many appointments, and I wasn't sure I would acclimate to it easily. I was wrong. I was a natural at driving the van! It was easier to drive than any vehicle I had ever handled. There were four side mirrors, a large rearview mirror and a backup camera. I saw the road much easier being so high off the ground, and I felt like I had become a better driver because of it.

The blessings of the Lord continued to be *poured* over our family. We had gained two more sons, a brand-new vehicle, and soon we were to have room for everyone in our new house that was *still* being built. But for now, we would endure in our three-bedroom, one-bath, house with all nine of us. It was cramped and I found it difficult to share one bathroom, but I couldn't help counting my blessings.

CHAPTER 19

Robert and Jordan

Robert and Jordan didn't come without their challenges. Aubrey and Aunna experienced less attention as Alan and I were required to prioritize who needed us most. Aubrey began acting out negatively to divert us, and Aunna would use missing her birth mom as an excuse to pull my attention towards her. I often would quickly validate their feelings of abandonment; however, we needed to help other children who had been in their situation to become better, happier, and stable just like they were. They understood the reason, but it didn't stop them from missing some of our involvement in their lives.

Robert blamed Jordan for the move again. He was happy to be living with his siblings, but was sick of moving. He felt it was Jordan's fault Michelle and Octavio sent them to live with us. He told me he understood the reason we gave—we wanted them to be with their siblings. However, he seemed to not understand why they couldn't be together in Michelle and Octavio's home. He wasn't willing to accept that he wouldn't have to move again. We told him we wanted to adopt him and we didn't want him to move again. The eye rolls, scoffs, and tears seemed to indicate he didn't believe us. He tested us by raising his voice, arguing, and lying. Alan and I tried to be patient. We continued to use the behavior chart as a reward system. It helped him understand our rules quickly and he made an effort to obey them. It also helped control his outbursts, but every time the topic of adoption came up, he tensed up and stared at the floor. I wondered if he continued to disbelieve what we had told him.

Jordan was a mystery. He was sweet, sensitive, and thoughtful towards others. He would genuinely care about people and their feelings; although, he had the capability to be the opposite too. He would yell, throw tantrums, argue, and purposefully say hurtful things to incite us. I couldn't understand how he could be so delicate one minute, and so senseless the next. His outbursts most often being the result of some correction. Jordan's self-image was not what it should have been. He loathed that he fell short of expectations, possibly due to years of verbal abuse from his birth parents. He requested, during the first week of living with us, to be sent to respite care, another foster home that temporarily cares for foster children with negative behaviors.

This was a common theme in his other foster homes. He would act up, and as consequence, would be sent to a respite home for a few days. I sensed that this was not what he needed now. He needed someone to show him love, regardless of the mistakes he made.

One night, after asking him to stop picking on his brother, he became angry. He yelled at anyone who dared speak to him or get in his way. He crossed his arms, squinted his face, and stomped as he paced around the basement playroom. I gathered the children and sent them upstairs to their bedrooms to avoid having them observe this episode. Swearing and self-harm were present, and I could not risk the other children trying to mimic this behavior. After distracting the children with activities and placing Faith in her swing, I went back to the playroom.

I found Alan calmly speaking with Jordan. Jordan was using his coping skills he had learned to calm himself; however, Jordan begged to be sent to respite. We told him that we didn't do that. No matter what choices he made, he wasn't leaving this house. He stomped his feet and stormed around the room grunting and crossing his arms. "Send me to Home of the Innocents!" he pleaded. He wanted us to send him to a nearby children's shelter. He wanted to be anywhere but here—with us. We told him that he was staying. We loved him and wanted him home. He was part of this family and he wasn't going to be sent anywhere. He sat on the floor and cried.

Alan walked over and, after a minute, asked if he could hug him. Jordan allowed it. In that moment I knew what we were doing was right. We were meant to parent him. Jordan deserved parents that wouldn't give up on him, that wouldn't send him away, and would give him the unconditional love all children are entitled to.

These episodes didn't last forever. After a few months, Jordan's petulance, for the most part, disappeared. Both Robert and Jordan sensed that they could trust us. We kept our promises to them and that simple act alone built a foundation that helped them adjust quickly into our family.

One evening Robert opened up about the previous homes he had lived in, he made the comment, "I feel loved here. There is always someone to play with and I feel like you listen to me." He noted that we valued, respected, and heard his opinion. He could feel our love for him. That was different about our home compared to others.

I have learned from experience that "the study of the doctrines of the gospel [of Jesus Christ] will improve behavior quicker than a study of behavior will improve behavior."[29] Michelle and Octavio had taught the boys well. They had done Bible studies together and taught them about the Savior, His atoning sacrifice, and why it was needed. With them knowing those truths, it

---

[29] Packer, Boyd K. "Little Children." *Ensign*. November 1986. p17. https://www.churchofjesuschrist.org/bc/content/shared/content/images/gospel-library/manual/09411/09411_000_089_handout.pdf. Retrieved from web 19 November 2019.

allowed Alan and I to expound upon what they already understood. We taught them the purpose of life: where we came from, why we are here, and where we are going after we die. The Lord has revealed, His purpose "[is] to bring to pass the immortality and eternal life of man."[30] We taught them this purpose and through His Plan of Salvation, they had the ability to become exactly like our Heavenly Father. They eagerly accepted these teachings and had many questions concerning religion, the Savior, and priesthood authority. It was stunning to see the change in them as they understood the gift of repentance, and used it daily. Their behaviors transformed. Their positive characteristics began to shine through. Their countenance changed from sullenness and anger to happiness and joy. They learned who they were, and that the Lord had a special mission for them. They had been given opportunities that most kids in their situation don't receive. They cherished the doctrine of Christ. They had learned first-hand the difference of living with and without it. They felt the joy that came from living a Christ-centered life.

Every child in our family improved beautifully with the gospel as their guide. They grew "in wisdom and stature,"[31] much like the Savior did. I could see their divine potential. Aubrey grew more obedient, service-oriented, and loving as she fell into her role as a big sister. Aunna became more helpful. She looked for needs

[30] Moses 1:39

[31] Luke 2:52

at home and asked if she could help fill them, like doing the dishes, mopping the floor, or distracting a toddler. Rae and Faith met all their developmental milestones and were discharged as patients from neonatal care. There weren't any indicators or effects from the drugs they were addicted to at birth or from being in foster care— more blessings from the Lord.

Despite the progress that we witnessed, I was still worried about Camden. He continued to have tantrums, but only after parent visits. Tiffany reiterated to me her thoughts often: This behavior was likely to continue until the judge ordered visits to stop. Camden's lack of listening or following directions would likely continue as well. Tiffany told me Camden wasn't sure which set of parents he should obey. Things were unstable and Camden needed *one* set of parents.

I rejoiced when the day of their termination hearing came. I met with Sara and the children's guardian ad litem outside the courtroom to go over what to expect during the hearing. I was nervous and calmed myself by texting my mother. I knew I would be hearing many injustices done to these children and I wasn't sure I had prepared myself mentally enough to hear them. The children's guardian ad litem questioned me about birth parent visits, the children's behaviors after visits, and what strategies Alan and I had used to help them cope. She double checked her notes to make sure no important details were left out during the hearing.

The double doors to the courtroom opened and
our case was called inside. Sara asked me to sit in the back
while she continued toward the plaintiff table. I
watched the children's birth mother enter with her
Cabinet appointed lawyer; the children's birth father
hadn't bothered to show up. The judge entered the
courtroom and we arose as she took her seat in the front.
I took my seat watching her closely. I wondered if the
rumors I had heard about her were true. Would she be
sympathetic towards these birth parents again?

I listened to the Cabinet present all of the
information collected in the span of six years. It was
horrible to listen to the many abuses that had been done
to the children. I was saddened by the many
opportunities, given by professionals and the court to
help the birth parents, that were not taken. I know that
Heavenly Father loves all His children, so it was
disheartening that these parents would not help
themselves. I genuinely felt sorry for them. Yet, through
this termination, I would be able to add their children to
my family. I loved each child and wanted to count them
as my own.

Three hours passed and finally all the arguments
were presented, counterarguments made, and witnesses
had testified. It was then I saw the truth of those rumors
concerning this judge. She pulled her hair up in a
ponytail as she deliberated upon the evidence presented.
It seemed obvious to me: Parental rights would have to
be terminated. My jaw dropped slightly at her next

statement, "Have we given her enough time? I mean, we are talking about a woman and her kids! Is there some rule of law that we can use to help this [birth] mother?"

She scrolled through lists of laws on her computer. I sat bewildered as I realized the judge had not prepared adequately enough for this hearing. She had been given the casefile and it had been in her possession a week prior to the hearing. It contained every argument and evidence that had just been presented during the proceedings. I sat speechless as she looked up the laws broken by the evidence collected by the State! Even worse, she was trying to find any reason to delay termination! This judge had already postponed this decision *years* beyond federal guidelines. I couldn't believe it.

The judge decided she would deliberate further on this case and have a decision to us in two weeks' time. I left the courtroom stunned. Sara assured me that while things did appear to be in favor of the birth mother, the evidence could not be ignored. This judge would have to terminate sooner or later.

I endured visitation through October and November while the judge deliberated termination—much longer than her promised two weeks. I knew I had to be patient. Their birth dad stopped coming to visits, so they became somewhat better, but were still emotionally draining. Birth mom acted like there was nothing abnormal about her situation, like nothing serious was happening. She continued to come to visits, Rae and Faith would still cry, and Camden still threw his weekly tantrum. Birth mom seemed to believe the "pro-parent" judge was somehow going to tip the scales in her favor. After all the birth parents had done, it was frustrating to think about the judge working so hard to find a loophole in the law that would allow them to keep the children.

About mid-December, I was cleaning the kitchen when my phone buzzed on the counter next to me. Glancing over to see who it was, I saw Sara's name on the screen. I quickly pulled up the text message. I stared confused as emojis of party hats and confetti cannons burst across the first few lines. Then I read the words I had longed for: Sara had received the official order from the judge. Rights had finally been terminated. I gaped at the screen for a few seconds and let the words wash over me. Years of abuse, unkept promises, and fear of the future came to an abrupt end. I no longer had to exhaust my physical and mental strength fighting for these children. Even more, the children no longer would have to suffer from the confusion of multiple people assuming the role of their parents. They were going to be mine. Tears welled up in my eyes and I couldn't help but jump excitedly around the kitchen.

Rae, Camden, and Faith came scurrying over to see what the commotion was about. I grabbed them into a tight hug and we danced and giggled. They didn't understand why mommy was so happy. They were going to be my babies forever. The Lord had spared them from a life of continued heartache and abuse. I prayed to thank God for being mindful of my children.

CHAPTER 20

A House and a Home

Building a house, going through visitation, dealing with resulting behaviors, and termination had been stressful on both Alan and I. We had difficulty sleeping due to the anxiety each issue gave us. In my case, it had led to severe migraines. It was the end of December, over a year since we had signed our contract, and the house we were building was still incomplete.

We had spent almost three months cramped in our little house. Looking back, it was a miracle that we fit three boys into a 10'x10' room with a desk, dresser, bookshelf, and a triple bunk bed—who knew those existed! All four girls had been stuffed tightly into the largest bedroom of the house, yet their beds were placed end to end and poor Faith was stuck in a pack-n-play behind the rocking chair in a corner—the only place for her to sleep in a room with three other girls. It was exasperating to everyone. Waiting for the bathroom and nearly cold showers were common. The bathroom needed to be cleaned almost on a daily basis with so many people using it. We needed a larger house and I was running out of patience.

Our builder should have had our house completed the previous Spring. I was living out of boxes and had been for six months! We were expecting a call to schedule a closing date, yet problems with workmanship kept pushing us back.

The builder sent Alan an email pressuring us to close on the house sometime before January and promised to have the final work done to perfection in a week's time. As much as I wanted to just sign the contract so we could move, it didn't sit right with me. We were spending a pretty penny on this house, far more than we would have preferred; we needed it built sturdily, correctly, and presentably. The tile in one bathroom still needed re-done and the wood floors weren't level, which we confirmed when we placed a ball-bearing on the floor and watched as it rolled to the other side of the room on its own. Beyond that, the ceiling in the master bath dipped to one side—which was obvious from the unevenness of the tilework on the shower walls—and the fireplace was four inches too low which caused problems when the builders tried to install the hearth. These things did not seem suitable for a home that is supposed to be new.

We confronted the builder; they needed to fix those issues before we could sign anything. We were spending too much money to not get the product we agreed to in the beginning: a solid, structurally sound, and cosmetically appealing home. They didn't care. They needed the payout. They had held onto the house for too long and it was causing a financial strain on their company. In their final email to settle with us, the builder gave us two options: We could either find a way to close by the 31st of December, for which they would provide us a $1,500 credit, or we could dissolve our contract and they would refund us our hefty, five percent deposit. Failing to choose by the end of business that day, however, would mean the builder would exercise their right to impose a $200 per day delayment penalty until closing.

Alan and I were shocked. We only had a few hours to make a decision. We could keep the house we were building, or accept their offer to cancel. As tempting as it was to keep the house, we decided to pray to find out what the Lord would have us do; it was a difficult choice to make. I had been looking forward to living in this beautiful home designed with finishes we had chosen. However, the contractor had not been pleasant to work with and didn't seem to care that much about the structure or finishing touches.

In hindsight, I can't imagine they truly considered the full weight of what they had offered us: a way to get out of our contract without any financial loss to us.

Like so many other times before, the Spirit answered our prayers. We felt that warm confirmation in our hearts to accept the refund and walk away. However, that decision came with the uncertainty of no longer knowing where we would find a more suitable space for our large family. I was disappointed, but I trusted in our revelation and the Lord. We moved forward with faith.

Alan got off his knees and I watched him silently pull up the internet on his phone. With the weight of the answer we had just received on his mind, before contacting the builder to cancel our contract, he decided to research homes for sale in the area of Louisville we desired to live. Wondering why this was his immediate response after our prayer, I asked him what he was doing. He calmly responded, "If I can just find something that *could* be appropriate for our family, that will give me the strength I need to call the builder and tell them of our decision."

His search didn't last long. Miraculously, the first home that Alan came across piqued his interest. The listing had six bedrooms, five bathrooms, a finished basement, double the square footage of our current new-build, but was about twelve percent more expensive. Based on the images, I was hesitant because it seemed like it needed a lot of work for the price. Alan later explained that in that moment he felt the pacifying influence of the Spirit; his anxiety was lifted. Even if this listing wasn't our future home, he knew the Lord had a plan for where we would live.

I took care of the children while Alan made a phone call to our mortgage lender. He wondered if we would qualify for a larger loan. After running some numbers, our lender approved us. If it wasn't for the experience of building, we would have never considered increasing our loan amount; we had added many upgrades to the home being built to make it comfortable enough for our family and were maxed out at the top of our price range. The listing Alan saw would need a little work, but it did contain the types of upgrades we had added to the new build. The answer was spiritually and logically clear: If we could purchase a house like this—with more square footage, and at a better price per square foot—it reaffirmed the revelation we had received moments before. It was decided and decided again: We would not follow through with purchasing the newly built home. When the builder didn't answer our call, we immediately sent an email asking to refund our money and cancel the contract.

We assumed the builder believed that in our minds, we had put in too much time, too much effort, too much stress, and wouldn't want to walk away from the beautiful home we had built with them. Before seeking the Lord's guidance, we had felt that way ourselves. Our sales representative for the building company called us later shocked and confused. He wanted to understand why we had backed out. He had been waiting to collect his commission from our house for over a year and had sacrificed much of his time to please us. We felt guilty; none of the delays or dissatisfaction throughout the process had been his fault. Yet, we had pulled a huge dollar amount right out of his pocket! Regardless, no matter what promises he made to convince us to proceed, we were not swayed from the decision we had made. We were acting in faith, trusting that the Lord would prepare a way for our family to find the right home.

The following day was the day before Christmas Eve. We met our realtor at the listing we had seen the day before. She appeared excited about this house. It was exactly what we had been looking for. We were surprised at the work the seller had already put into it. He had hired painters to paint the walls at the same time we arrived to view the listing. The color happened to be the exact same color we had picked out for our new build. He had cleaned the house from clutter and mold due to it being a foreclosure that he had purchased recently. Due to personal reasons, he had decided to flip the house and resell it.

We imagined ourselves living in the house. We measured the empty spaces in the kitchen where appliances should have been. We discovered that the ones we had purchased for our new build would also fit in this kitchen. Off the kitchen, on the main floor, housed the master bedroom and other common areas. Those were isolated from the other bedrooms in the house.

We realized quickly that we could easily separate the children too. Upstairs, there were two bedrooms with a jack-and-jill bath and double vanities; we imagined the girls would share this space. There was also a guest room with its own private bathroom. Downstairs was a walk-out basement with an additional two bedrooms, bathroom, and large play area for the boys. There was even some unfinished space for storage or to be finished and added to the square footage later. Everyone had the potential to be separated into their own areas. Everything seemed too perfect.

This house coming on the market, at the same time we were required to drop our contract, was no coincidence. We were sure. We put in an offer and it was accepted the same day. It was another blessing that proved our Heavenly Father was mindful of our family and was "prepar[ing] every needful thing; and establish[ing] a house"[32] perfectly fitted for us.

---

[32] Doctrine and Covenants 88:119

CHAPTER 21

Time and Eternity

The past few years have consisted of highs and lows. Each bump along the way we pushed through with a love of the Savior, trust in His plan, and faith. The culmination of events, small and great, that led us to adopt these children was my "refiner's fire."[33] I relied on the Holy Ghost and used His influence to help direct me in all the choices we made. No matter how difficult things turned out to be, we endured them with faith. We had aligned our will to the Lord's; the return we received in blessings for having a "broken heart and contrite spirit"[34] has been more than I could have imagined.

Christmas was enjoyable and Alan and I relaxed a

[33] Malachi 3:2

[34] 3 Nephi 9:20

little knowing we had a solid plan for our family after the holidays. However, Sara had postponed the children's final birth parent visit until after Christmas break. Her hope was that the children wouldn't associate Christmas with losing their parents. I acknowledged her sentiment and understood her reasoning.

The first Monday after school started back, we gathered together one last time at Sara's office. I took a deep breath in the car and thought "Once more, and then no more." I got out of the side of our fifteen-passenger van and went around to unload the children. Their birth mother was waiting for us in the playroom. Birth dad had refused to come, but I was relieved he had refused. It would make it easier on the children.

Rae held tight to my legs while Faith clung to my neck—as they had done every week for a year. They again protested being left with their birth mother. I handed Rae a toy to distract her and Sara took Faith. I quickly ran out of the room and closed the door behind me. I could hear their screams echo all the way down the hallway as I exited the building. "One more time. I just have to do this one-more-time," I repeated these words to ease the tug on my heart.

A few minutes later, Sara texted me to come back inside. Wondering why she had made an unusual request, I quickly rushed back to the playroom. Their birth mother was sitting on the floor next to Faith who was still crying. She reached for me as I entered the room. Rae was sulking in a corner and rushed to my side also. Their birth mother looked up relieved that I had returned. "Will you stay with us?" she asked. I was surprised. This was her goodbye visit! It would be the last time she would see her children! Surely, she didn't want me interrupting this time? I looked at Sara who nodded from across the room.

"Sure," I smiled and sat down on the carpet next to Faith. Rae sat next to me and I pulled some blocks towards the girls. We quickly built towers and knocked them down. Camden came over to join us in our fun. The boys had been kicking a ball around on the opposite side of the room together.

Their birth mom leaned over and said, "Thank you. I just didn't want them to cry the whole time." I responded that I understood and kept playing with the kids. I let her have opportunities to build towers for Camden, Rae, and Faith to knock down. We encouraged Robert and Jordan to come build with us. It was a memorable moment as we played with one another on the floor. It seemed like a torch was being passed— children were handed from one mother to another.

The hour ended, and we took a picture with their birth mom. After she helped me ensure all the children had put on their coats, we hugged and waved goodbye, and headed out the back door to the van. Robert and Jordan wept. They loved their mom. However, they knew they were better off with Alan and I. I could see their struggle because they didn't fight it. They left obediently with me; both silently helped me buckle the babies in their car seats.

Before we had made it out of the parking lot, Sara called my phone. "Thank you for doing that."

"No worries," I replied.

"She was hysterical before the visit started. She really struggled with doing this goodbye visit and you made it easier for her," Sara told me. I hadn't realized the impact I had on their birth mother.

"Really?"

"Yes, you have always treated her like a real person and she appreciated that. She told me she was happy that her kids are together, they are happy, and that *you* will adopt them. She really likes you." Sara helped me recognize that the meekness and humility I had shown their birth mother was what had helped her cope with her situation. It had given her the courage to accept what was best for her children. It had given her the peace needed to move forward with her life—knowing her kids were going to be okay. There was no resentment or hostility. I was thankful that we were able to have peace between us. Kindness had won.

***

We closed on our house at the end of January. I spent that week cleaning and prepping for our move the following Saturday. The Lord was keeping his promises. Things were becoming better with each passing day and month. Many people worked behind the scenes to make this transition exciting and less worrisome. The school district worked to create a bus route for the boys, so they would not have to change schools mid-year. The State workers helped us speedily accomplish a new home-study to quicken our adoption.

By spring, the State issued us an adoption worker who immediately began the paperwork on our family. To her surprise, the children's presentation summaries, the file presented to the adoptive family, were complete. Someone had done their paperwork already without this caseworker's knowledge. People I had never met before were working tirelessly to give these kids a forever home, *my* home. I again counted my blessings.

I contacted the adoption attorney we had used twice before with Aubrey and Aunna. He was surprised to hear we were adopting again—and not one, but five more children! He accepted our case happily and took care of the legal portion of our paperwork.

By June we had an adoption court date: July 21, 2019. We entered the courtroom that day in matching Team Alami t-shirts with our names printed on the back and a number in the order the children came to us: Aubrey (1), Aunna (2), Rae (3), Camden (4), Faith (5), Robert (6), and Jordan (7). We all sat tightly around two tables in the middle of the courtroom. Our family, friends, Michelle and Octavio, and even Sissy came to witness the adoption.

During the proceedings, we were questioned by the judge about how we would care for several children. Our response: We had made it work thus far. The older kids had eagerly stepped into their older sibling roles and helped. We loved them and were nurturing love between them. We were ready to officially be pronounced a family.

The judge looked down at her casefile. Her face hardened and she seemed unsatisfied with what had happened in this case. She had been there for every hearing, had tried to find many loopholes for their birth parents, and had unwisely allowed visitation to continue no matter what the cost to these precious children.

I wondered what she was thinking. Why did she hesitate to make this moment the happiest for these children? The events that led them to adoption, were in the past. We needed to give these children stability and a happy home.

She didn't look up, but simply said, "Okay." It was anticlimactic for everyone present. However, that one word meant a great deal to us. It sent Jordan into silent tears. For him, it was over. No more moving about. No more anxiety about his future. It was settled. He had a family who loved him. He was home. I rubbed his back and hugged him tight. The weight was lifted. This burden that he had carried for so long was gone in a matter of seconds. He had gone through a refining of his own. All these children had. It had taken so much faith in the Savior to get to adoption day. I will never forget the tears I shed nightly for each of my children. Now, they were "swallowed up in the joy"[35] that all of them were legally mine.

We celebrated with pizza and arcade games at a restaurant called Gatti-Land. I enjoyed each moment with my newly adopted children. We tired ourselves out with play and then quickly drove to the church for the baptism of Robert and Jordan. It was a lot to do in one day, however Robert and Jordan eagerly and earnestly desired to be baptized. They had waited patiently; now that they were adopted, they didn't have to wait any longer. Additionally, Alan and I desired to go to the temple and seal these children ours for time and all eternity as soon as we could. Robert and Jordan had to be baptized first in order to accomplish this goal.

Robert and Jordan had a wonderful baptism with

---

[35] Alma 27:17

many familiar faces to
greet them and witness
their special day. They
were dressed in white and
the happiness of the day's
events shone from their
faces. Robert came up out
of the water and he told

me he felt "like [he] was on fire." He knew the Lord had
been mindful of him and had brought him to us. He
expressed how he felt the Holy Spirit confirm that he
was doing what the Lord required of him. I was proud of
these boys. Robert and Jordan's choices had led them to
have faith in Jesus Christ, repent, and follow the Savior's
example to be baptized. I rejoiced in their righteousness.

A few days later, on Saturday, July 27, 2019 we
gathered to the Louisville Kentucky Temple to be sealed
as a family. Everyone was dressed in white. The children
waited with their grandmothers in the front foyer as
Alan and I went back to the sealing room. I sat staring at
the altar of the temple. This was the moment that was
most important to me. I wanted my kids for time and all
eternity. Adoption simply made them legally mine for
this life, sealing them would make them mine *forever*. I
smiled at Alan. We would be adding five more to our
eternal family.

Those we invited took their seats in the sealing
room to witness the ordinance. Both my mother and
mother-in-law walked in holding hands with several

children. Each child nervously watched and waited for instructions. Alan and I knelt on opposite ends of the alter and gathered the children to  kneel around it as well. We placed Faith on the top so that Alan or I could hold her and keep her calm while the sealer used his priesthood authority to bind our family on earth and in heaven.[36] He recited the prayerful words of this sacred ordinance beautifully. I wept as I thought about every struggle we had faced. Every trial, heartache, and loss endured was culminated as we were sealed around that alter, linked together for eternity.

I glanced at Rae across from me. I could have never imagined the impact one little girl would have on our family. Rae was a miracle. She had brought us all together. The love I felt for my baby girl had carried over to infinite love for her siblings. I said a prayer of gratitude to the Lord, thanking him for this beautiful child who had entered our lives. I marveled at how deeply I loved these children. I wouldn't have fully understood this without our experience of loss with Rae.

In the bible, Peter teaches, "that the trial of your faith, being much more precious than of gold that

---

[36] Matthew 18:18

perisheth, though it be tried with fire, might be found unto praise and honour and glory at the appearing of Jesus Christ."[37] As I mentioned before, I would have given up all of my material possessions for Rae when the State decided to take her. She was much more precious to me than gold. I was humbled the Lord brought her back to me, and revered the opportunity to be a mother to her and her siblings. The testimony I gained from this experience carries me daily. I have learned, "I am a child of God. His promises are sure. Celestial glory shall be mine if I can but endure."[38]

I know that the Savior, Jesus Christ lives. I trust and have faith in His promises. They are real and certain based on our faithfulness. Our family was built through His divine intervention. I have seen the workmanship of His hand in my life and the lives of my children. He knows and is mindful of all His Spirit children; He knows each strength and weakness. He knew the challenges that I would face on this earth. Line upon line, he revealed what was required of me and sent His Spirit to guide and sustain me along the way. As I put aside my will, and chose to do His will in His way, I saw miracles in His time. We have been given the invitation, "come unto Christ, and be perfected in him, and deny yourselves of all ungodliness; and if ye shall deny yourselves of all ungodliness, and love God with all your

---

[37] 1 Peter 1:7

[38] Randall, Naomi Ward. *I Am a Child of God.* 1978

might, mind and strength, then is his grace sufficient for you, that by his grace ye may be perfect in Christ; and if by the grace of God ye are perfect in Christ, ye can in nowise deny the power of God."[39]

It has been said, "Hindsight is 20/20." After sharing a picture of us holding Rae on the first day she came into our lives, Michelle once asked us, "knowing what you know now, what would you tell your younger self that day?" Alan and I agree: Enduring and experiencing the pain, the joy, and the miracles that have happened— with advanced knowledge—it would be harder to see the hand of God. There is no doubt in my mind that God orchestrated the events. Everything that has happened has given us knowledge, experience, and spiritual growth that is only attainable by having gone through it. For the sake of all this, I wouldn't tell myself anything.

[39] Moroni 10:32

Bibliography

1   From *A Child's Prayer* © 1984 Janice Kapp Perry. Used by permission.
2   'Gospel Topics, 'Patriarchal Blessings', https://www.churchofjesuschrist.org/study/manual/gospel-topics/patriarchal-blessings?lang=eng, (25 January 2020).

3   Doctrine & Covenants 3:1

4   James 4:10
5   1 Nephi 3:7
6   Matthew 6:19-20
7   Matthew 19:14
8   'Well-Known Expressions', *Book Browse*, https://www.bookbrowse.com/expressions/detail/index.cfm/expression_number/586/if-at-first-you-dont-succeed-try-try-again, (7 October 2019).
9   Doctrine and Covenants 90:24
10 'Well-Known Expressions', *Book Browse*, https://www.bookbrowse.com/expressions/detail/index.cfm/expression_number/586/if-at-first-you-dont-succeed-try-try-again, (7 October 2019).
11 Neal A. Maxwell. *Brim with Joy*. Brigham Young University devotional address. 23 January 1996. p2. https://speeches.byu.edu/talks/neal-a-maxwell/brim-joy/
12 James 5:14
13 Daniel 4:35
14 Spurlock, Janie. Personal Journal. 13 May 2017.
15 Spurlock, Janie. Personal Journal. 13 May 2017.
16 Alma 17:9
17 Text: Ruth M. Gardner, 1927–1999. © 1980 IRI Music: Vanja Y. Watkins, b. 1938. © 1980 IRI https://www.churchofjesuschrist.org/music/library/hymns/families-can-be-together-forever?lang=eng&_r=1
18 Philippians 4:13

19 1 Nephi 1:20

20 D&C 105:18-19

21 1 Nephi 3:7

22 Johnson, Peter M. *Power to Overcome the Adversary.* Ensign. November 2019. p110.

23 Malachi 3:10

24 Doctrine and Covenants 64:34

25 *The Family: A Proclamation to the World.* 1995. Retrieved from web 4 December 2019.
    https://www.churchofjesuschrist.org/topics/family-proclamation?lang=eng&old=true

26 John 16:33

27 1 Corinthians 10:13

28 Matthew 5:11-12

29 Packer, Boyd K. "Little Children." *Ensign.* November 1986. p17.
    https://www.churchofjesuschrist.org/bc/content/shared/content/images/gospel-library/manual/09411/09411_000_089_handout.pdf.
    Retrieved from web 19 November 2019.

30 Moses 1:39

31 Luke 2:52

32 Doctrine and Covenants 88:119

33 Malachi 3:2

34 3 Nephi 9:20

35 Alma 27:17

36 Matthew 18:18

37 1 Peter 1:7

38 Randall, Naomi Ward. *I Am a Child of God.* 1978

39 Moroni 10:32

Made in the USA
Columbia, SC
07 June 2024

36780202R00104